D1266788

THE BIBLICAL MEANING OF MAN

THE BIBLICAL MEANING OF MAN is one of the IMPACT BOOKS, a series designed to bring the modern reader the significant achievements of scholars, both Catholic and non-Catholic, in the fields of Scripture, Theology, Philosophy, Mathematics, History, and the Physical and Social Sciences. Among the titles in the series are:

THE
Biblical Meaning
of Man

DOM WULSTAN MORK, O.S.B.

THE BRUCE PUBLISHING COMPANY / MILWAUKEE

IMPRIMI POTEST:
> GERALD BENKERT, O.S.B.
> Abbot

NIHIL OBSTAT:
> JOHN A. SCHULIEN, S.T.D.
> Censor librorum

IMPRIMATUR:
> ✝ WILLIAM E. COUSINS
> Archbishop of Milwaukee
> March 10, 1967

Library of Congress Catalog Card Number: 67–21898
© 1967 THE BRUCE PUBLISHING COMPANY
MADE IN THE UNITED STATES OF AMERICA

FOR MY ABBOT,
THE RIGHT REVEREND GERALD BENKERT, O.S.B.

Contents

Introduction

This book could well have for its subtitle: Biblical Anthropology, or even Biblical Psychology. It is, for the most part, a monograph on the biblical view of man as flesh-soul-spirit.

I say "for the most part" because the book sharply divides into two sections. The first is a research-work which, after a general survey of the biblical teaching on man, studies the meanings of "flesh," "soul," and "spirit" as these terms relate to man in the Old and New Testaments. One chapter on the Spirit of God in the Old Testament has been included for the better understanding of the spirit of man. I have studied every text in the Bible relating to these three aspects of man in the Hebrew and Greek versions, and have consulted most of the literature on the subject. The result is a monograph which I believe is quite comprehensive.

My intention here has been to fill a real need for a work that presents not just the Old or New Testament teaching on man, or the view of one biblical writer, but the view of the whole of biblical revelation. I have followed the gradual process of revelation, and have, as much as possible, presented man as the Bible presents him in that evolving process. It follows that I have let the biblical texts speak for themselves. The statements of authorities quoted serve only as commentary on the texts.

The last two chapters make up a second section, dependent on, yet separable from, the previous eight. They are conclusions, or corollaries, essays in which I have attempted to make the biblical view of man relevant to contemporary man. These are "fighting" chapters, for some will not agree with my conclusions, especially those in the last chapter. A good way of beginning this book for many would be to turn to the second section first.

Biblical man, hence man as he is revealed in the Bible, is a unity of flesh, soul, and spirit, not a trichotomy, nor a dichotomy of body and soul. The Hebrews saw man whole, a healthy viewpoint for balanced, integral living, and radically related both to God, mankind, and all of creation. We need this viewpoint today, to counteract a still-lurking Platonic attitude, and to correct a too natural, secularized, acceptance of the human situation.

I have written this book mainly for those who are in a position to influence others. It is vital at any time, but especially today, to know what man is. Those who receive the Bible as God's revelation can only interpret man as God does so consistently throughout the whole Bible. If God reveals man as flesh-soul-spirit, then that is what man is. What these three aspects are, and what the biblical meaning of man is, comprise the task for this book.

May it be of help to teachers, especially teachers of theology, the Bible, philosophy, psychology, and the social sciences. May it assist priests and ministers to indicate man's being and destiny to those to whom they are committed. May it call the attention of those engaged in psychological research and therapy to the biblical notion of man's spirit, that aspect of every man that naturally relates him to God. Students will, I hope, find the first eight chapters a handy source of references.

This book has been a labor of love, growing into a compulsion. What began as research for my own information has developed into a monograph. I am grateful beyond words to those who had a part in it in any way.

I single out for particular gratitude my Abbot, the Rt. Rev. Gerald Benkert, O.S.B., who first interested me in the biblical meaning of man, who gave me permission to write the book, and who has always shown the greatest interest in its progress. The dedication of the book to him is a small repayment. The headmaster of Marmion, the Rev. Joseph Battaglia, O.S.B., and the Dean of Studies, the Rev. René Cyr, O.S.B., have graciously and fraternally made working conditions possible in the midst of my duties in the school. Mr. William E. May of the Bruce Publishing Company is an editor whose erudition and insight greatly improved the manuscript. His suggestions have been those of a consultant rather than of an editor. This is my third book which Mrs. Carl Berkhout has prepared for the press, and with a self-lessness that has always edified. Mr. Robert Allenson loaned valuable books from his own personal library. The libraries of Bellarmine School of Theology and McCormick Theological Seminary have been hospitable and indispensable. But my greatest debt to a library is to that of Bethany Theological Seminary and its librarian, Mr. Marlin Heckman. Bethany has always welcomed me to an excellent collection in a most conducive setting. To all of these I am especially grateful.

In the creation account in Genesis, we read that God spoke, "And it was so." Not so in the account of his creation of man. There he breathed into dust, and the result was a *nephesh*, a man. This, then, is biblical man: the dust of the earth, the breath of God — a person.

THE BIBLICAL MEANING OF MAN

CHAPTER 1

The Biblical Doctrine of Man

The Bible reveals the relationship of God and man to each other. This relation results from the redemptive act of Christ. The Bible indeed reveals God as he is in himself, but this revelation is not academic but functional: it presents God always in relation to the redemption of man. As Geerhardus Vos has worded it: "Revelation is the interpretation of redemption. . . ."[1]

The word of God reveals what the God-and-man relationship is to be: an intimate union of Person with person. Its basis is covenant: God revealing and man accepting — "All that the Lord has spoken we will do" (Ex 19:8); "But all who received him, who believed in his name, he gave power to become children of God" (Jn 1:12). When God reveals himself on his side of the covenant it is for the purpose of man's response on his side. The end, then, of this revelation is union, and this end determines its mode. It is true that God is being-from-himself, all powerful, infinitely perfect; but he is all this as outgoing Love, which creates, and freely chooses, loves, and forgives — as Love willing union with the person it has created. And that person is seen in the Bible as created for union, by a likeness to God that seeks union with like, with the breath of God within him acting as a link between them.

---

[1] Geerhardus Vos, *Biblical Theology* (Grand Rapids: Wm. B. Eerdmans Publishing Company, 1963), p. 14.

BIBLICAL MAN

We would look in the Bible in vain for the tracts *De Deo Uno et Trino* and *De Homine*, although systematic theology builds on what the Bible reveals about God and man. God is presented there in relation to man; and man, in relation to God. Likewise we will not find in the Bible a professed anthropology or psychology. Although each of these disciplines has its own autonomy, the man of faith must, to complete the description they provide, view man according to his revealed nature and destiny, and take as normative the human conduct that results from covenant.

The Bible does not ignore man as man, nor does it simply presume that he is a *human* being, with human needs, desires, relationships, and never refer to these. The Bible knows that man is what he is and provides for his humanness: a man marries, produces children, *enjoys* the "good life," rules, works, and appreciates nature. Biblical man is not an ascetic who lives almost exclusively in the soul. He is a real man, alive, who enjoys living, too much so at times.

And that is another feature of biblical man: he is not presented to us in the abstract, nor even, with rare exceptions, as a fictional person. No; he is a real person, be he Abraham, or Moses, or David, or Elijah, or Paul, or Christ. Père Gélin wrote: "Jesus is the biblical man par excellence. . . ."[2] Biblical man is alive. Much instruction which could have been presented abstractly is packed into parables: "Or what woman, having ten silver coins . . ." (Lk 15:8); "There was a man who had two sons" (Lk 15:11). The persons in the parables may be fictional, but they soon become real when the reader identifies them with people he knows. The Wisdom literature comes to us, as it were, in human form. For example, self-restraint is advised by, "When you sit down to eat with a ruler, observe carefully what is before you; and put a knife to your throat if you are a man given to appetite" (Pr 23:1–2). Moral teaching becomes incarnated.

---

[2] Albert Gélin, S.S., *The Religion of Israel* (New York: Hawthorn Books, 1959), p. 109.

In the Bible we see man in every human activity. We are even quite aware of his anatomy, even if the Jews were not too precise about it and assigned psychological functions to physical organs. The heart, for example, was considered the seat of determination, also of thought — among several other human actions.[3] Language can be sensual to a degree that to us sounds daring. For instance, the "love of God and man for each other" is a very abstract and dry way of putting things. It takes life in, "kiss me with the kisses of your mouth!" (SS 1:2.) That's the point — religion takes life in the Bible, because God is revealed as alive, active; and man is portrayed as alive, very much human, and very much a part of his human situation. Biblical man is hardly the product of "angelism."

G. C. Berkouwer has made some excellent observations that are pertinent here:

"We may say without much fear of contradiction that the most striking thing in the Biblical portrayal of man lies in this, that it never asks attention for man in himself, but demands our fullest attention for man in his relation to God. We can doubtless characterize this portrayal as a religious one. With this term, we do not at all mean to imply that Scripture has no interest in man's various cosmic and interhuman relationships. The opposite is unquestionably the case. . . . When we speak of the demand for full attention to man's relation to God, we do not mean to relativize all his other relations; but it appears again and again that the relation to God is of decisive and all-inclusive character in these other relationships. For man's relation to God does not exclude these other relationships as unimportant, but rather implies the utmost importance of these other relationships. . . . The characteristic of the Biblical view lies precisely in this, that man appears as related to God in all his creaturely relationships. . . . The man of God is man in this relation, from which we may never abstract him. This is man as he makes his way through the world, not enclosed in himself, not independent and autonomous, but as man of God."[4]

[3] Cf. H. Wheeler Robinson, The Christian Doctrine of Man (Edinburgh: T. and T. Clark, 1947), pp. 11–14, 22–24.
[4] G. C. Berkouwer, Man: The Image of God (Grand Rapids: Wm. B. Eerdmans Publishing Company, 1962), pp. 195–196.

"Consequently," writes the Anglican bishop of Woolwich,

"all words pertaining to the life and constitution of man are to be seen as designating or qualifying this fundamental relationship of man to God. The parts of the body are thought of, not primarily from the point of view of their difference from, and interrelation with, other parts, but as signifying or stressing different aspects of the whole man in relation to God."

As to the confusion about the scientific nature of man which I mentioned above, Bishop Robinson continues:

"The Hebrew had little or no interest or competence in psychology or physiology. But that must not blind us to the fact that there is in the Old Testament a profound anthropology or doctrine of man. All the richness of Semitic terminology in respect of the body and its functions was devoted to expressing a deep understanding of the *theological* truth of man's nature."[5]

It is the theological truth about man which the Bible presents, not the physical, sociological, or aesthetic — certainly not man as an isolated person, abstracted from God and fellow-man, man *in se*. The Bible in revealing man as a relation to God takes a far more realistic view of man than do the various academic disciplines. The healing sciences, psychology, sociology, the arts, and other academic subjects treat either of a part of man, or of penultimate ends. Only revelation grants these ends, takes into consideration all of the parts, and gives ultimate purpose to the whole man.

COMMUNITY AND INDIVIDUAL

Bernhard Anderson has resolved the tension for biblical man between community and individual:

"In the biblical view, man is truly a person only when he stands in a community — in relationship to God and to his fellow man. When he is isolated from the community, like Cain in his banishment, he suffers the greatest loneliness and misery."[6]

---

[5] John A. T. Robinson, *The Body: A Study in Pauline Theology* (London: SCM Press, 1961), p. 16.

[6] Bernhard W. Anderson, *Understanding the Old Testament* (Englewood Cliffs, N. J.: Prentice-Hall, Inc., 1964), p. 370.

This sounds very much like William H. Whyte's "together-ness" — the group is more important than the individual — and indeed it is really that, but with the important distinction that the individual is still responsible for his own salvation.[7]

Biblical man can never be separated from the covenant people. God's election is first of his people, his covenant is with them, and his revelation is to them. We can see this better if we consider the difference between public and private revelation: the first is to God's people, the second is to an individual person, not necessarily to be transmitted to the people as a whole. The Jew is of importance because he is a Jew, because he belongs to the chosen people. In this sense the group is more important than the person. Under the new covenant the group becomes the body of Christ, and the individual is only a part of it, a membrane, useless apart from the whole Christ.

When God speaks to Moses from the burning bush, he refers to Jacob's descendants as "my people," and to himself as "the God of your fathers, the God of Abraham, the God of Isaac, the God of Jacob" (Ex 3:6–7, 10, 13, 15–16). Formed more immediately in Egypt, the Israelites formally become God's people by the covenant at Sinai. God's first concern is with them as a group: "Thus you shall say to the house of Jacob, and tell the people of Israel . . ." (Ex 19:3–4); "You shall be to me a kingdom of priests and a holy nation. These are the words which you shall speak to the children of Israel" (Ex 19:6). Throughout Israel's history the people as such come first; they act together, the word of God is given for them. For example: "And Samuel said to all Israel . . ." (1 S 12:1); "And David and all Israel went up to Baalah, that is, to Kiriath-jearim which belongs to Judah, to bring up from there the ark of God, which is called by the name of the Lord who sits enthroned above the cherubim" (1 Ch 13:6); "Thus says the Lord: Behold I will restore the fortune of the tents of Jacob. . . . At that time, says the Lord, I will

---

[7] Cf. William H. Whyte, Jr., The Organization Man (New York: Simon and Schuster, 1956), p. 47.

be the God of all the families of Israel, and they shall be my people" (Je 30:18; 31:1). The Jew would never be able to conceive of the individual simply as individual. He was first one of God's people, an Israelite.

H. Wheeler Robinson originated the expression "corporate personality," by which he meant that the Israelites had a far deeper sense of community than we do today. He meant that the Israelite sees his family, his clan, as well as his nation, as a single person of which he is only a part. The whole is the person. One result of this mentality is that a member of a clan, for instance, can be substituted for another: the clan is one large personification, and conversely, it is totally present in each of its members. This concept was not exclusive with the Israelites, but common to their neighbors in ancient times, as is witnessed by the Code of Hammurabi.[8] Robinson adduced as proof of corporate personality such instances as a three-year famine which Israel had to suffer for Saul's slaughter of the Gibeonites. The atonement which the remaining Gibeonites demand of David is also proof of this primitive concept of family solidarity: "Let seven of his sons be given to us, so that we may hang them up before the Lord at Gibeon on the mountain of the Lord." The seven whom David gives over to them are not Saul's children but grandchildren. Thus the innocent must atone for the sin of their grandfather (2 S 21:1–9). For the same reason Jehu kills Joram, Ahab's son, because Ahab had at least permitted Naboth's murder (1 K 21:1–16; 2 K 9:24–26). In the decalogue God says: "For I the Lord your God am a jealous God, visiting the iniquity of the fathers upon the children to the third and fourth generation of those who hate me, but showing steadfast love to thousands of those who love me and keep my commandments" (Ex 20:5–6).

An early example of levirate marriage is that of Onan and Tamar: "Then Judah said to Onan, 'Go in to your broth-

---

[8] Cf. H. Wheeler Robinson, op. cit., pp. 8, 27–30; also the same author's *Corporate Personality in Ancient Israel* (Philadelphia: Fortress Press, 1964). Cf. Gn 20:7–9; 26:10 for instances of "corporate personality" for non-Israelites.

er's wife, and perform the duty of a brother-in-law to her, and raise up offspring for your brother' " (Gn 38:8). This type of marriage is later legislated in Deuteronomy: "If brothers dwell together, and one of them dies and has no son, the wife of the dead shall not be married outside the family to a stranger; her husband's brother shall go in to her, and take her as his wife, and perform the duty of a husband's brother to her. And the first son whom she bears shall succeed to the name of his brother who is dead, that his name may not be blotted out of Israel" (Dt 25:5–6). Here is proof of the concept of family solidarity, by which one person can substitute for another with no thought of unreality in the arrangement. It is interesting here to note Deuteronomy 24:16, where we see a breakdown in this concept: "The fathers shall not be put to death for the children, nor shall the children be put to death for the fathers; every man shall be put to death for his own sin." By the time this was written, individualism had developed, with the sense of personal responsibility. Still, as we see from the legislation for levirate marriage, the idea of corporate personality was an essential element of Jewish thinking.

The Jews were constantly conscious of their solidarity as God's covenant people. They were, after all, made blood-brothers by Moses' sprinkling on them blood from the sacrifice that sealed the covenant: "Behold the blood of the covenant which the Lord has made with you in accordance with all these words" (Ex 24:8). The covenant would be renewed and with it the sense of solidarity: "And Jehoiada made a covenant between the Lord and the king and people" (2 K 11:17); "And the king [Josiah] stood by the pillar and made a covenant before the Lord, to walk after the Lord and to keep his commandments and his testimonies and his statutes, with all his heart and all his soul, to perform the words of this covenant that were written in this book; and all the people joined in the covenant" (2 K 23:3). National solidarity could account for the fall of Jerusalem and the end of the kingdom: "We acknowledge our wickedness, O Lord, and

the iniquity of our fathers, for we have sinned against thee"
(Je 14:20). That we encompasses the whole of Israel, past
and present, and the innocent ones in the present have sinned
in the sins of their ancestors.

One person alone can personify the whole group, somewhat as an ambassador is his country. This is especially true
of the king: he, of all his people, is his people. We have already seen this in the case of a famine which the Israelites
have to endure because of Saul's sin. The people also suffer
a pestilence that takes seventy thousand because David's pride
prompted him to order a census (2 S 24:1–17). We have seen
both Jehoiada and Josiah making a covenant with God that
is, in reality, a covenant between the people and God. "The
covenant between Yahweh and Israel and between Yahweh
and David is one and the same thing," writes Sigmund
Mowinckel. The same author is able to explain some of the
"I" psalms by this facet of corporate personality: "Likewise,
the priest or the king contains the whole and all its members,
when he appears as the leader of the cult. He really represents
— in the old meaning of the word — the whole people. When
he says 'I' it is the whole Israel who speaks through him and
who appears in his person 'in the presence of Yahweh.' "[9]

Yet it could be that the very personality of the king — his
own, that is — gave great impetus to individuality. Great men,
such as David and Solomon, personalities in their own right,
embodying in their greatness, not in their sins, all of the de-
sirable qualities of the true Israelite, then add the glamorous
features of the daily life of an oriental potentate — here were
incentives to be a person such as these. One has only to recall
the poor queen of Sheba with "the wind knocked out of her"
at the heady experience of Solomon and all his glory. For
the Israelite, it was an easy transition from "That's how I'd
like to live!" to "That's what I'd like to be!"

Of course the sense of individuality is older than that.
Walther Eichrodt writes:

---

[9] Sigmund Mowinckel, *The Psalms in Israel's Worship* (Nashville: Abingdon Press, 1962), Vol. I, p. 44.

"The Book of the Covenant, Ex. 20–23, which goes back at least to the time of entry into the promised land, and codifies still earlier customs, gives us a valuable insight into the relation between the protection afforded by the Law to the community as a whole, and the claim made on the Law by the individual."[10]

However, each of the Israelites is responsible for keeping the covenant, and it is this that argues an early concept of individuality. The people of God is made up of persons, upon each of whom is given the duty of the commandments. The very matter of the commandments embraces details of personal life: honoring a definite father and mother, not coveting a neighbor's house or his wife. The response to these is personal, and it springs from, as it expresses, a personal love of God: " . . . those who love me and keep my commandments" (Ex 20:6. Cf. 20:1–17).

Personal responsibility is seen in the laws of Exodus 21–23. They treat of persons — a kidnapper, a man burning his field, a man who borrows an animal — and presume individual, not group, acting and thinking.

Outside influences, especially Greek, helped to make the Israelite realize that he was an individual, but the greatest impetus to a full sense of his own responsibility was the preaching of the prophets. They were, according to Père Gélin,

". . . pioneers in the matter of religious individualism. When their religious experience is studied in their most typical representatives, it emerges as a personal communion with God. Jeremiah's 'confessions,' which so often alternate with his prophecies, are a good example of this."[11]

The prophet is a man of God, in contact with him, with the result that he himself emerges more Godlike than others. Since one of the basic facts which God reveals about himself

---

[10] Walther Eichrodt, *Man in the Old Testament* (London: SCM Press, 1961), p. 10. Eichrodt here stresses individual responsibility, and this emphasis serves as a corrective to a too enthusiastic reception of "corporate personality." He differs from Robinson also in his *Theology of the Old Testament* (Philadelphia: The Westminster Press, 1961), Vol. I, p. 483 n.

[11] Albert Gélin, S.S., *The Key Concepts of the Old Testament* (New York: Paulist Press, 1963), pp. 66–67.

in the Old Testament is that he is personal, the prophet understood this more deeply, and took on something of the personality of God. "The process by which the prophet came to reflect the thought and feeling of God exalted him into a new consciousness of individual worth to God."[12] Made in the image of God, all men are therefore persons. But the prophets built up a sense of individuality more by their demands. The Israelite cannot hide behind the nation, claiming his privileged status of belonging to the people of God as substitute for his own inactivity: "Behold the days are coming, says the Lord, when I will punish all those who are circumcised" (Je 9:24). The worship of the temple, highly organized, ritualistic, so much of which was liturgy by the group, was also something the Israelite could participate in — ex opere operato — and feel that he was discharging his duty to God as a faithful Israelite, even though he was burning incense to Baal on the side. Jeremiah blasts this mentality: "Hear the word of the Lord, all you men of Judah who enter these gates to worship the Lord. Thus says the Lord of hosts, the God of Israel. Amend your ways and your doings, and I will let you dwell in this place. Do not trust in these deceptive words: 'This is the temple of the Lord, the temple of the Lord, the temple of the Lord!' For if you truly amend your ways and your doings, if you truly exercise justice one with another . . ." (Je 7:2–5).

Here is a clear example of the tension between community and individual. The temple worship, which had become "the reduction of religion to a mass affair by means of a refined exercise of the cult," emerged after the exile as the most outstanding expression of Israel's group consciousness.[13] When a Jew was part of the great religious festivals at Jerusalem he realized that he was one of the people of God, he identified with something larger than himself, and could, if he were lax in his observance of the law, nonetheless feel that he was a good Jew merely because he was one. The case re-

---

[12] H. Wheeler Robinson, Corporate Personality in Ancient Israel, p. 29.

[13] The quotation is from Walther Eichrodt, Man in the Old Testament, p. 21.

sembles that of a Catholic who goes to Mass only at Christmas and Easter — he feels an identification with the Church that is somehow going to save him without his own efforts. Jeremiah resolved the tension by giving the people these words of God: "For in the day that I brought them out of the land of Egypt, I did not speak to your fathers or command them concerning burnt offerings or sacrifices. But this command I gave them, 'Obey my voice, and I will be your God, and you shall be my people; and walk in all the way that I command you, that it may be well with you'" (Je 7:22–23). Samuel had said the same thing to Saul: "Has the Lord as great delight in burnt offerings and sacrifices, as in obeying the voice of the Lord? Behold, to obey is better than sacrifice, and to hearken than the fat of rams" (1 S 15:22).[14]

Individuality in the context of sacrifice is beautifully expressed in two psalms. First, in David's psalm of repentance: "For thou hast no delight in sacrifice; were I to give a burnt offering, thou wouldst not be pleased. The sacrifice acceptable to God is a broken spirit; a broken and contrite heart, O God, thou wilt not despise" (Ps 51:16–17). The meaning here is that a sacrifice which is not prompted by sincere interior dispositions is useless. But note the personal, individual, dispositions which God demands! The following passage from Psalm 40 is applied by the author of Hebrews to Christ: "Sacrifice and offering thou dost not desire; but thou hast given me an open ear. Burnt offering and sin offering thou hast not required. Then I said, 'Lo, I come; in the roll of the book it is written of me; I delight to do thy will, O my God; thy law is within my heart'" (Ps 40: 6–8. Cf. Heb 10:5–7). The sacrifices of the people of God, simply because they belong to that people, have no meaning apart from the fundamental union of the individual's will with the will of God. This mentality carries right on down to Christ, who is the perfection of biblical man.

Christ denounces over-optimistic dependence on corporate

---

[14] Cf. Is 1:11; Ho 6:6; Am 5:21–27; Ec 4:17.

personality.[15] For instance, he says " . . . many will come from east and west and sit at table with Abraham, Isaac, and Jacob in the kingdom of heaven, while the sons of the kingdom will be thrown into the outer darkness . . ." (Mt 8:11–12). The reason for their exclusion is their lack of personal faith. St. John the Baptist earlier attacked the same mentality: "and do not presume to say to yourselves, 'We have Abraham as our father'; for I tell you, God is able from these stones to raise up children to Abraham. . . . every tree therefore that does not bear good fruit is cut down and thrown into the fire" (Mt 3:9–10).

This linking of personal retribution to personal responsibility in the New Testament had its origin in prophetic preaching. And as revelation about an after-life became more definite, so did individuality become more defined. "Already there was a growing conviction that the sense of fellowship which they enjoyed with God in this life could not surely come to an end with death, but that even in Sheol men might be able to praise him. With this there was growing up in Israel a new conception of religious individualism, associated particularly with Jeremiah, a man of deep personal religious experience. This emphasis was continued by Ezekiel who coupled with it a doctrine of individual retribution which declared that men are punished in proportion to their sin and rewarded in proportion to their righteousness during their lifetime here upon the earth."[16]

Ezekiel, especially, stressed individual as against corporate responsibility: "The righteousness of the righteous shall be upon himself, and the wickedness of the wicked shall be upon himself" (Ezk 18:20); "Therefore I will judge you, house of Israel, every one according to his ways, says the Lord God" (Ezk 18:30). However, reward for Ezekiel can be summed up by *life*, and punishment, by death (Cf. Ezk 18). *Life* for him means continued earthly existence, and death, a termination of the same, with no consideration given

---

[15] For Christ's acceptance of corporate personality cf. Mt 10:41.

[16] D. S. Russell, *Between the Testaments* (Philadelphia: Muhlenberg Press, 1960), p. 15.

to reward or punishment after death. Job's case is an apparent contradiction to this: his afflictions are to all appearances a punishment from God for his sins. In this state he can hardly be said to be *living*. Yet he sees a personal reward and vindication after death: "For I know that my Redeemer lives, and at last he will stand upon the earth; and after my skin has been thus destroyed, then from my flesh I shall see God, whom I shall see on my side" (Jb 19:25–27).[17]

In Isaiah 26:19 occurs what can be taken as the first expression in the Bible of the resurrection of the dead: "Thy dead shall live, their bodies shall rise. O dwellers in the dust, awake and sing for joy!" These are the just or righteous (Is 27:7). The wicked, however — "they are dead, they will not live; they are shades, they will not arise; to that end thou hast visited them with destruction and wiped out all remembrance of them" (Is 26:14). A general resurrection of both good and bad is stated in Daniel: "And many of those who sleep in the dust of the earth shall awake, some to everlasting life, and some to shame and everlasting contempt" (12:2). Reward and punishment are actually eschatological, as they are in every case dependent on what the individual has made of his favored position as one of God's people. Hence, to repeat, as revelation about an after-life becomes more definite, so does individuality become more defined.

Biblical man is both corporate and individual, or, rather, he is a responsible individual who is a part of the group, whose responsibilities derive from his membership in the group. Membership can never cancel responsibilities; instead it causes them. But the idea and fact of corporate personality is good and necessary in view of the whole Christ, his body. Gélin wrote in this regard:

"In the religious field, the old ideas [about corporate personality] lasted longer. Does this merely imply the obstinate survival of a traditional way of thought? I should prefer to say that the idea of solidarity, provided it was subject to criticism, correction and refinement, was obliged to persist in view of

---

[17] Cf. R. H. Charles, *Eschatology* (New York: Schocken Books, 1963), pp. 61–73. This is a reprint of a standard work first published in 1899.

the future work of Christ, who was one day to achieve our salvation by summoning all people to the bosom of the community of the children of God."[18]

THE WHOLE MAN

"Any attempt at a successful interpretation of the Bible," Aubrey Johnson writes,

"seems bound to take note of the fact that Israelite thinking, like that of the so-called 'primitive' peoples of the present day, is predominantly synthetic. It is characterized by what has been called the grasping of totality. Phenomena are perceived for the most part as being in some sort of relation. . . ."[19]

Thus man is seen in the Bible as whole. There is no dividing him into body and soul, or body, soul, and spirit. Man divided against himself is straight Platonism, it is never the thought of revelation. The dichotomy of body and soul either springs from or ends up as body versus soul. The body conceived as the prison of the soul — a concept which has done so much harm to Christian spirituality — is Platonic, not Christian, and certainly not Hebrew. St. Francis' "Brother Body" agrees with the biblical viewpoint, but never his earlier "Brother Ass."

It is tempting to say here that biblical man is a unity of body and soul, as against a dichotomy, but while nearer the truth, it would still not be the truth, and at the beginning it is vital to start out right. Rather, biblical man is simply a unity. This unity is viewed from three different aspects — "flesh," "soul," and "spirit." These three are not substances — the Hebrew would not think this way — although as revelation progresses and with it a belief in life after death, it rather looks as if the soul and body could be considered as such. However, the Hebrew concept of the disembodied soul

---

[18] Albert Gélin, S.S., *The Key Concepts of the Old Testament*, p. 66. The very fact that the effects of the original sin of Adam persist in his descendants derives from corporate personality. Cf. J. De Fraine, S.J., *Adam et Son Lineage* (Brussels: Desclée de Brouwer, 1959), p. 223. The whole book is a study of corporate personality in the Old and New Testaments.

[19] Aubrey R. Johnson, *The Vitality of the Individual in the Thought of Ancient Israel* (Cardiff: University of Wales Press, 1949), p. 7.

is that it is basically only an aspect of the dead person, so that life after death has to be that of the resurrected body. The notion of the soul set free from the body by death and at last being able to live is certainly not biblical. Life for biblical man is that of his person, and that necessarily includes his "flesh." The best illustration of this mentality is the passage in Genesis that describes the creation of man: God breathed into the dust which he had formed, " . . . and man became a living soul" (Gn 2:7, Conf. tr. The RSV uses "being" for "soul"). (Soul here is not quite the best translation of the Hebrew nephesh, but it will do for a starter.) If man is a soul, then his body is also his soul, and that is precisely what the passage is saying. The soul is visible in and through the body. It is the life aspect of the person, and when the person walks, a spectator sees the soul, that is, a living person.

E. C. Rust has strikingly illustrated the Hebrew attitude. The body and soul (nephesh) "were different aspects of the same physiological and psychical whole. We cannot speak as if the nephesh uses the hands or the feet, the mouth or the ears, for in a very real sense the nephesh is at that moment the hands, feet, mouth or ears. . . . When a man heard, the ear was for that moment the active aspect of the whole, and could stand for the soul."[20]

I have referred already to the confusion of the physiological and the psychical in biblical man. Regarding this, Claude Tresmontant writes that in the Bible " . . . because there is no dualism, passions, organic functions, sensations, are just as easily related to the soul as they are to the organs and, conversely, thoughts and sentiments are ascribed to the organs and to parts of the body."[21] This procedure is a good deal closer to present-day psychosomatic medicine than is Greek dualism.

If relationship is a key to understanding the Hebrew mind,

[20] E. C. Rust, Nature and Man in Biblical Thought (London: Lutterworth Press, 1953), p. 114.
[21] Claude Tresmontant, A Study of Hebrew Thought (New York: Desclée Company, 1960), p. 100.

and, therefore, the Bible, it is basic for grasping man as he is presented to us in the Bible. Here parts are so vitally related to each other, so overlap in function, that they demand us to see man whole. This whole man is not alone, but is related to the nation, which, in turn, is related to God. Relating does not come easy to our Graeco-Roman mentalities (with Persian influences, such as an ever persistent Manicheism). We have a penchant and a genius for dividing, whether in philosophy, organizations, education, sciences, or arts. We want to analyze, and then isolate, hoping eventually to synthesize. The Hebrew contemplates an object, which means that he looks at it much as a baby does, not analyzing it, but seeing it whole. We sit down and listen to a symphony, and at once are looking for form — themes, development, restatement; the Hebrew would simply enjoy its beauty. We must approach the study of biblical man as a Hebrew, that is, we must see him already synthesized.

That is my procedure in this book. We shall study man from the biblical viewpoint. Therefore we shall see him from his three aspects of flesh, soul, and spirit. While at first glance this looks like analysis, we must keep in mind now and throughout our study that under each aspect we are viewing man whole: man as flesh, man as soul, man as spirit. Thus, even though we consider man as flesh, soul, and spirit in turn, we are always considering him as a synthesis.

Some introductory remarks on terminology are in order. The Hebrew word for flesh is *bashar;* for soul, *nephesh;* and for spirit, *ruach.* The Greek words respectively are *sarx, psychē,* and *pneuma.* Apart from chapter headings I shall often refer in this study to these Hebrew and Greek terms rather than to their usual translated meanings. The reason for this will soon be evident, namely, that *bashar, nephesh,* and *ruach* cannot validly be translated simply by flesh, soul, and spirit. Moreover, what we mean by flesh, soul, and spirit doesn't quite match the biblical reality. It is best, until we realize the full biblical meanings, to drop these words — which have their own Western contexts and connotations — and stay with the Hebrew and Greek. Thus we will be better able to preserve our minds from conceptual prejudices.

In proof of this, and of the necessity of such a study, let me ask, what does Christ mean by "God is spirit" (Jn 4:24)? A person who is not conversant with the meaning of spirit as applied to God in the Old Testament would answer that God is not a material substance. True, but this is very Greek and not very biblical; hence it is miles from what *Christ* means. Or what does St. Paul mean by his famous clash of flesh and spirit in Galatians 5:17? He is *not* speaking of the opposition of body and soul.

We must *understand* what the Bible tells us about man, for this, after all, is God's revealed word. We hear and read this word, but we don't understand. It is absolutely necessary, if we are to know what we are, to know what God says we are.

Therefore we must turn to a deep study of biblical psychology, to the three aspects of man signified by *bashar, nephesh,* and *ruach.* When we read God's word again, we shall know what we are, where we fit in, and where we are going.

Only the man of revelation has relevance for our times, because only he is man as man basically is. Only when we know man as *bashar, nephesh,* and *ruach* can we ask Freud, Jung, and Harvey Cox what they have to contribute.

Paul van Buren, in a recent interview, said: "I would want to say that Christianity, around the figure of Christ — a considerably reinterpreted figure, I would have to admit — has developed a certain image of man and of human relationships. These can also be, and have been, developed in the Western humanistic tradition. Whether and to what extent this humanism was influenced by Christianity is perhaps a secondary question."[22]

As soon as we look at man "as he is in himself" we have succumbed to this humanistic tradition — man as man, abstracted from God and fellowman. Such an approach might

---

[22] Ved Mehta, "The New Theologian," *The New Yorker* (Nov. 13, 1965), p. 153.

have been valid for the Greeks, but it can never be valid for the Christian. Whatever the image of man and his relationships may as a fact be at present — derived from the Renaissance, and before that from Greek philosophy — they must yield to an image of man which the Bible presents. This image is of man as *bashar* and *nephesh* — a human person, bound-up with his fellow humans, very much alive on, and radically part of, this earth; and as *ruach* — just as radically bound-up with and oriented toward God. *Humanistic* Christian man is "man in himself," body and soul, to whom the supernatural comes as a sort of gift, a super-addition. Biblical man cannot possibly exist apart from a natural aptitude for union with God, which is realized in Christ. If Christian man has failed in the West, it is because he has seen himself as more Greek than biblical. And if Christianity seems irrelevant to "the secular city" it is because Christian man has not understood what he is.

Christian man, biblical man, is ultimately Christ, as the corporate personality of the people of God is in reality the Person of the incarnate Son extended and continued in his body the Church. Biblical man, therefore, is a relation to Christ, and he is fulfilled by being "in Christ," as Paul puts it. But even Christ is in relation to the Father as his Son. The final end of the whole Christ is the Father in a union that is trinitarian: "That all may be one, even as thou, Father, in me and I in thee; that they also may be one in us . . ." (Jn 17:21). Let history vindicate the truth of the biblical concept.

CHAPTER 2

Flesh

It is unfortunate that *bashar* and *sarx* have been translated
so often by "flesh" in the English versions of the Bible — via
the *caro* of the Vulgate — for the word "flesh" bears connotations that are undesirable. First of all, it smacks of im-
morality: "sins of the flesh" invariably means sinful indul-
gence in sex, or, at least, in drinking. The reason for this is
that "flesh" is generally a synonym for the body, and the
body, according to the influential streams of Platonism, Jan-
senism, and Puritanism, running through so much of our
religious writings down the centuries, is bad, or, at best,
suspect. It is true that "flesh" in the Bible does not represent the highest and noblest aspect of man; St. Paul, especially, inveighs against it. Yet it is not the body which is
being condemned, but man, the whole man, in his natural-
level, earthbound, propensities. To straighten out Christian
spirituality, it is imperative to straighten out the Christian
view of man. Hence we must carefully study the biblical
view, and begin with man at his most creaturely level, that
of his "flesh," or *bashar*.

BASHAR-SARX IN THE OLD TESTAMENT

1. *The Body*

Bashar occurs 266 times in the Hebrew Old Testament.
One of its most common meanings is bodily substance, the
"stuff" of which the body is composed. An example of this
is Genesis 2:21–24: "So the Lord God caused a deep sleep to
fall upon the man, and while he slept took one of his ribs
and closed up its place with flesh; and the rib which the
Lord God had taken from the man he made into a woman

19

and brought her to the man. Then the man said, 'This at last is bone of my bones and flesh of my flesh. . . .' "[1] In Ezekiel's vision of the dry bones, God spoke to them through the prophet: "I will lay sinews upon you, and will cause flesh to come upon you, and cover you with skin . . ." (37:6). Two other instances from many others[2] can be cited: "And this shall be the plague with which the Lord will smite all the peoples that wage war against Jerusalem: their flesh shall rot while they are still on their feet, their eyes shall rot in their sockets, and their tongues shall rot in their mouths" (Zc 14:12). "They have given the bodies of thy servants to the birds of the air for food, the flesh of thy saints to the beasts of the earth" (Ps 79:2).

The Septuagint translates bashar in the above citations (and those in note 2) by sarx. Because sarx is a most important word in the Pauline concept of man, it is chiefly this Greek rendering of bashar that interests us in this study. It is vital in understanding St. Paul's meaning of sarx to grasp its Old Testament meaning. The notion that Paul borrowed his opposition of sarx and pneuma — "flesh" and "spirit" — from Hellenistic thought has been refuted by W. D. Davies and others. We shall see from the concepts associated with sarx that Paul was a Hebrew of the Hebrews.[3]

Definitely bashar-sarx denotes the substance of bodily flesh, the material element of man. But we find bashar also used to mean the flesh-meat of animals. While the Septuagint renders it at times by sarx,[4] it more usually does so by kreas.[5]

However, according to the Hebrew mind, the substance of flesh is something that man has in common with animals;

---

[1] Unless otherwise noted all citations from the Old Testament are from the Revised Standard Version. Copyright 1952 by the Division of Christian Education of the National Council of Churches, and used by permission.

[2] Cf. 2 Kgs 4:34; 5:14; 9:36; Jr 19:9; Gn 17:11, 13, 14, 24; Nm 12:12; Is 49:26; Ezk 44:7; Jb 13:14; Zc 11:9.

[3] Cf. W. D. Davies, Paul and Rabbinic Judaism (London: S.P.C.K., 1962), pp. 17 ff.

[4] Gn 41:18; Lv 4:11; 17:14; 26:29. And note Ws 19:21.

[5] E.g. Ex 22:30; Dt 12:20, 23, 27; 14:8; Nm 11:4, 13, 18, 21, 33; Is 22:13; Jgs 6:19, 20, 21; 1 S 2:13, 15; Je 7:21; 11:15; Ezk 4:14; 11:3, 7, 11; Zc 11:16; etc.

or, as we shall see, it is more correct to say that man and animals are *bashar*.[6] The Genesis account of the flood bears this out: "For behold, I will bring a flood of waters upon the earth, to destroy all flesh in which is the breath of life from under heaven" (Gn 6:17); "Of every living thing of all flesh, you shall bring two of every sort into the ark . . ." (Gn 6:19); "Bring forth with you every living thing that is with you of all flesh — birds and animals, and every creeping thing that creeps on the earth . . ." (Gn 8:17); "This is the sign of the covenant which I have established between me and all flesh that is upon the earth" (Gn 9:17).[7]

Therefore *bashar* can also mean the human body, considered as composed of flesh, visible, external. Most of the time, in this connotation, the Septuagint translates it by *sarx*, less often by *sōma*. The latter is the Greek word for *body*, and is a key word in Pauline theology. Some instances of *bashar* as body, rendered by the Septuagint as *sarx*, are: "They [the priests] shall not . . . lacerate the body" (Lv 21:5; Conf. tr.). "I will remove the stony heart from their bodies . . ." (Ezk 11:19; Conf. tr.). " . . . my body dwells secure" (Ps 16:9).

Although *geviyah* and *gevah* both mean the body, *geviyah* is only used eleven times (including references to corpses), and *gevah* once, in the Hebrew Bible.[8] The body is generally represented by the wider term *bashar*.[9] However, this fact in itself does not prove that the ancient Jews did not consider the body as an entity, or, if they thought that way at all, as a substance. Besides, we are not interested here in the use of *bashar* in general, but in its biblical use, and we have seen

---

⁶ It is interesting to note the LXX translation of *bashar* as *kreas* in Jb 10:11, meaning bodily substance.

⁷ Cf. Gn 7:15, 16, 21; 9:11, 15; BS 13:16.

⁸ Cf. Ex 4:7; 30:32; Jgs 8:7; Lv 17:11; Ps 85:3. For *sōma* texts cf. Lv 19:28; Nm 8:7.

⁹ For *geviyah* cf. Gn 47:18; 1 K 31:10, 12; Ezk 1:11, 23. For *gevah* cf. Jb 20:25. For those interested in pursuing the subject, and Bishop John A. T. Robinson's implications, cf. his monograph *The Body: A Study in Pauline Theology* (London: SCM Press, 1961), p. 11 ff; also James Barr's criticism of the same in his *The Semantics of Biblical Language* (Oxford: University Press, 1962), p. 34 ff.

in the above citations that the Jews were well aware of their bodies and their fleshly substance. If we can deduce any conclusion so far as to the meaning of *bashar* with regard to man, it is that it stood for man as composed of flesh, which he has in common with the lower orders of animals, but which is completely subject to God. *Bashar* is created by God, and it can be destroyed and punished by him, as well as healed and restored. The meaning of the word is wide because of the Jews' wide comprehension of the reality. As Eduard Schweizer wrote recently:

> "The Hebrew, when speaking of man, by implication means man in the presence of God. . . . He is always 'flesh,' mere creature, absolutely dependent on God's strength, limited, mortal, threatened by illness and death. 'Flesh' in this sense is not a part of him, it is his very being, and never is he to forget that he is flesh for his whole life and in all his deeds and experiences."[10]

2. The Whole Man

If *bashar* can denote a relationship with the animal kingdom, *a fortiori* it is able to express human kinship: " . . . for he is our brother, our own flesh" (Gn 37:27); "Remember also that I am your bone and your flesh" (Jgs 9:2); "And now our flesh is as the flesh of our brethren, and our children are as their children" (Ne 5:5).

Bashar then can mean a kinship with the whole human race, a solidarity with the family of man, with which one has human "flesh" in common. Flesh as a bond of human solidarity is commonly asserted in the Old Testament. Witness the following passages: "God of the spirits of all flesh" (Nm 16:22; 27:16); " . . . for the Lord has an indictment against the nations; he is entering into judgment with all flesh" (Je 25:31); "And the glory of the Lord shall be revealed, and all flesh shall see it together . . ." (Is 40:5); "then I will pour out my spirit on all flesh" (Jl 21:28).[11]

---

[10] Eduard Schweizer, *The Church as the Body of Christ* (Richmond: John Knox Press, 1964), pp. 17–18.

[11] Cf. also Gn 6:12; Jr 45:5; Is 66:16, 23, 24; Ezk 21:4, 9, 10; Zc 2:17; Jb 34:15; Ps 65:3; 136:25; 145:21; 56:5; BS 14:17; 18:11; 41:4.

The Greeks expressed the solidarity of all men by the abstract term "human nature." This abstraction, however, would be foreign to the Hebrew way of thinking, which preferred the concrete term "flesh" to represent the bond linking all men.

Then there are texts wherein *bashar* (and in the Septuagint, *sarx*) stands for the whole man, not only man as fleshly, but also as rational, desiring, and feeling. Among these are the following: "O God, thou art my God, I seek thee; my soul thirsts for thee; my flesh faints for thee" (Ps 63:1); "My soul longs, yea, faints for the courts of the Lord; my heart and flesh sing for joy to the living God" (Ps 84:2); "Be not rash with your mouth [literally 'your flesh']" (Ec 15:2). All of the *kol bashar* texts referring to mankind refer to the whole man.

One use of *bashar* which we shall consider treats of the whole man, yet it adds a particular nuance to the biblical meaning of "flesh," for it connotes man's "nothingness" as flesh in the eyes of God. "If he [God] should take back his spirit to himself, and gather to himself his breath, all flesh would perish together, and man would return to dust" (Jb 34:14–15). "He [God] remembered that they were but flesh, a wind that passes and comes not again" (Ps 78:39). What is man in relation to God? Nothing. He is a creature, dependent for his being and continued existence upon God. "All flesh is grass, and all its beauty is like the flower of the field," said Second Isaiah (40:6). Man is mortal: "For who is there of all flesh, that has heard the voice of the living God speaking out of the midst of fire, as we have, and has still lived?" (Dt 5:26).

Man is utterly powerless against God: "In God I trust without a fear. What can flesh do to me?" (Ps 56:4); "The Egyptians are men, and not God, and their horses are flesh, and not spirit . . ." (Is 31:3).

In commenting on this latter passage, Walther Eichrodt distinguishes between spirit and flesh:

> " 'Spirit' is the inexhaustible power of the divine life, in which all life takes its origin; and *bashar* is the life of earth,

which is essentially transitory and, like everything earthly and created, exhibits no principle of life in itself. . . . The opposition between the permanent and the transitory world is in the last resort a conflict between the moral will which forms the world and that which is attached to egoistic and material ends."[12]

Bashar can connote an opposition between God and man, between the creator and the created, between the transcendent and the limited. It designates earthbound man, horizontal, akin to the "flower of the field," or "grass," at one with the dust from which he came. And we see a different kind of opposition in this passage from Jeremiah: "Thus says the Lord: 'Cursed is the man who trusts in man and makes flesh his arm, whose heart turns away from the Lord'" (17:5). Because of its natural endowments *bashar* can harbor a pride that is self-deceptive. Possessed of a certain strength, it can mistakenly rear up against God, trusting in a specious self-sufficiency. Because *bashar* — fleshly, earthly, visible, animal, and created — is what it is, it tends to break with the creator and to glory in its nothingness.

"In an important group of cases," wrote Wheeler Robinson,

" 'flesh' [*bashar*] is used of man, or man's essential nature, in contrast with God, or with 'Spirit,' to emphasize man's frailty, dependence, or incapacity . . . the contrast does not occur before Isaiah 31:3, and must not be read into the earlier Hebrew thought; its importance consists in its being the point of departure for the development of the Pauline doctrine of 'flesh,' with distinct ethical reference."[13]

SARX IN THE NEW TESTAMENT

We are aware by now that *bashar-sarx* has a number of meanings in the Old Testament. It is utterly false to think that there might be one meaning, or one that became more or less exclusive with the development of the word. In a

---

[12] Walther Eichrodt, *Theology of the Old Testament* (Philadelphia: The Westminster Press, 1961), Vol. I, pp. 215–216. I have changed Eichrodt's transliteration of *bashar* to conform to mine.

[13] H. Wheeler Robinson, *The Christian Doctrine of Man* (Edinburgh: T. and T. Clark, 1947), p. 25. This passage has been quoted in Davies, *op. cit.*, pp. 18–19.

study such as this there is the temptation to say that bashar shed its cruder connotations of bodily substance and flesh-meat with the centuries, but facts do not allow this. In later books of the Old Testament bashar is indeed used for both, and in the last book to be added — Wisdom — so is sarx. All of these meanings carry over into the New Testament, and if St. Paul develops one more than the others, he has not discarded them. They all give us God's revelation as to the meaning of man.

1. The New Testament Exclusive of St. Paul

Sarx means bodily substance in the words of Christ to the Apostles after the resurrection: " . . . a spirit has not flesh and bones as you see that I have" (Lk 24:39).[14] While "flesh" in the passage " . . . unless you eat the flesh of the Son of man and drink his blood, you have no life in you" (Jn 6:53; cf. 6:51–56) would seem to have the same meaning, actually it refers to Christ's body.[15] Raymond Brown, following Lagrange, is of the opinion that John 6:51–59 is out of context, and suggests that John actually incorporated here material taken from the Last Supper. This would account for his omission of the institution of the Eucharist. Hence "flesh" and "blood" in this particular verse mean the body and blood of the eucharistic sacrifice, blood having a specifically sacrificial connotation.[16]

In the following passage from Revelation we see that sarx can mean the fleshy substance common to men and animals: " ' Come, gather for the great supper of God, to eat the flesh

---

[14] Unless otherwise specified, the New Testament citations are from the Revised Standard Version. Copyright 1946 by the Division of Christian Education of the National Council of Churches, and used by permission.

[15] Sōma, body, does not interest us at this time. It was used by Paul, as we know, to develop his teachings on the resurrection of the body and the Christian's union with Christ. In the words of Bishop Robinson, Pauline sōma means "the external man," "the external presence of the whole man," "personality" in the philosophical sense, "the whole person." John A. T. Robinson, The Body (London: SCM Press, 1961), pp. 27–28.

[16] Cf. Raymond E. Brown, S.S., New Testament Reading Guide: The Gospel of St. John and the Johannine Epistles (Collegeville: The Liturgical Press, 1960), pp. 40–41. Cf. also Brown's The Gospel of John I–XII (Anchor Bible, Garden City, N. Y.: Doubleday, 1966), comment on Jn 6:59.

of kings, the flesh of captains, the flesh of mighty men, the flesh of horses and their riders, and the flesh of all men, free and slave, both small and great' " (19:17–18).

With the addition of pāsa (all), sarx designates mankind, the human race. "And if those days had not been shortened, no human being would be saved . . ." (literally "all flesh would not be saved") (Mt 24:22). "Thou hast given him power over all flesh . . ." (Jn 17:2). Luke quotes, with reference to John the Baptist's mission, words of Isaiah in which "all flesh" means all mankind; Peter on the day of Pentecost quotes Joel, who has the same meaning (Lk 3:6; Acts 2:17).

That sarx means human nature in the New Testament we also know from John's most famous line: "And the Word became flesh [sarx]" (Jn 1:14). Christ, in speaking to Nicodemus, considers it in the same way, but in contrast with spirit: "That which is born of the flesh is flesh, and that which is born of the Spirit is spirit" (Jn 3:6). He does this again later: "It is the spirit that gives life, the flesh is of no avail" (Jn 6:63). We have met this contrast between flesh and spirit before, in Isaiah 31:3, and have seen that it is a difference between the divine and the merely human. While reserving any further comments on spirit to the chapters on ruach-pneuma, I believe that the meaning of sarx in these two passages is human nature as such, what could be called natural man, considered in himself. We see this contrast — and meaning — again in Peter: "Christ . . . was put to death in the flesh but made alive in the spirit . . ." (1 Pt 3:18). Sarx in John 8:15 has the sense of human mode of acting: "You judge according to the flesh. . . ."

The often quoted sentence of Christ in the garden of Gethsemane, "The spirit indeed is willing, but the flesh is weak" (Mt 26:41), gives us a new aspect of sarx: as purely human it is naturally weak, susceptible to the demands of nature, prone to the easiest way.

But John takes this aspect a step farther: "If any one loves the world, love for the Father is not in him. For all that is in the world, the lust of the flesh and the lust of the eyes and the pride of life, is not of the Father but is of the world" (1 Jn 2:15–16). "Our fallen nature" aptly renders *sarx*, for John sees it not merely as weak, but as tending to evil. Peter takes the same view: "The Lord knows how to deliver the God-fearing from temptation and to reserve the wicked for torment on the day of judgment, but especially those who follow the flesh in unclean lust and despise authority" (2 Pt 2:9–10, Conf. tr.). Here is Arndt and Gingrich's comment on "follow the flesh" in their Lexicon: " . . . the *sarx* seems rather to be the power of the defiling desire, to which (*sarx*) the sinners have pledged allegiance."[17]

Sarx, then, has in the New Testament writers we have considered the same meanings that it had in the Old Testament, and we can conclude that so the word was generally understood. In its contexts it had for the New Testament Jew the same familiar connotations which it had in the Old Testament.

2. Sarx in St. Paul

"The question now arises how the Pauline view stands in relation to that of Jesus. Paul is, indeed, particularly important, for he is the only New Testament writer who to any great extent offers us direct statements about man's nature, and uses extensively the anthropological terminology of his time. Paul's anthropological statements have, therefore, always determined quite decisively the whole picture of man which Christian doctrine has extracted from the New Testament."[18]

Paul uses *sarx* 91 times, a frequency which derives from the word's importance in the development of his theology. We shall see this importance especially in the opposition of *sarx* to *pneuma*.

Paul's use of *sarx* to signify bodily substance is negligible and mainly refers to circumcision; for example: " . . . nor is that man circumcised who is so outwardly, in the flesh" (Rm

---

[17] William F. Arndt and F. Wilbur Gingrich, *A Greek-English Lexicon of the New Testament* (Chicago: The University of Chicago Press, 1963), p. 578.
[18] Werner Georg Kümmel, *Man in the New Testament* (Philadelphia: The Westminster Press, 1963), p. 38. Kümmel's study of Christ's view of man is mainly from sources other than those we are considering.

2:28, Kleist-Lilly tr.). *Sarx* can mean the "outer man" in the sense that a man is visible, tangible — his external aspect.[19]

It also expresses kinship: " . . . in the hope that I may provoke to emulation those who are my own flesh . . ." (Rm 11:14, Kleist-Lilly tr.); "Consider Israel according to the flesh" (1 Co 10:18). *Sarx* also stands for the wider kinship of humanity, mankind: "For no human being [*pāsa sarx*] will be justified in his [God's] sight by works of the law" (Rm 3:20); " . . . a man [*pāsa sarx*] is not justified by works of the law" (Gal 2:16).

Therefore it is to be expected that Paul uses *sarx*, as does the Old Testament, for human nature. Abraham is "our forefather according to flesh" (Rm 4:1); " . . . flesh and blood cannot inherit the kingdom of God . . ." (1 Co 15:50); "by abolishing in his flesh the law" (Eph 2:15); "Slaves, obey in everything those who are your earthly masters [*kata sarka:* masters according to the 'flesh']" (Col 3:22).[20]

There is nothing peculiarly emphatic about *sarx* as designating the natural level in Paul. Here, as elsewhere, it means the *merely* human order as against the divine. "Let no one disqualify you . . . puffed up without reason by his sensuous mind" (Col 2:18). The Greek has "being puffed up by the mind of the flesh." This passage clearly indicates the fact that Paul, following the common Hebrew concept, considered *sarx* as capable of expressing the whole man, albeit the whole natural man. The "flesh" is not only bodily substance, but also mind. The RSV's translation of "the mind of the flesh" as "sensuous mind" delineates the sphere of the "sarkical" intellect. An example of natural-level thinking is seen in this passage: "Do I make my plans like a worldly man [*kata sarka*], ready to say Yes and No at once?" (2 Co 1:17.) Here is another: " . . . not many of you were wise according to worldly standards [*kata sarka*]" (1 Co 1:26). Natural-level motivation is also conveyed by *kata sarka:* " . . . acting in worldly fashion" (2 Co 10:2).

---

[19] Cf. Col 2:13; Eph 2:11.
[20] Cf. 2 Co 10:3; Gal 2:20; Eph 6:5; Heb 2:14; 10:20; 12:9.

Paul's doctrine of the enmity between flesh and spirit is based radically on the difference between the two. This difference is that which exists between two orders: the merely human, or natural, and the divine. This is brought out neatly in this passage: "So, for my part, brothers, I could not treat you as spiritual persons: I had to treat you just as creatures of flesh and blood [*sarkinois*], as babies in Christian living. I fed you with milk, not solid food, for you were not ready for it now, for you are still worldly [*sarkikoi*]. For when there are still jealousy and quarrels among you, are you not worldly [*sarkikoi*] and living on a merely human level [literally: according to man]?" (1 Co 3:1–3. The translation is that of Goodspeed.) The fleshy, *sarkical* level of living, one quite different from the level of spirit, has its own standards, and these are the standards of the world, the horizontal world of the *sarx*, arising from and grounded in self. "Jealousy and quarrels" are usual *sarkical* conduct. In Romans 8:5–8, Paul writes: "For those who live according to the flesh set their minds on the things of the flesh, but those who live according to the Spirit set their minds on the things of the Spirit. To set the mind on the flesh is death, but to set the mind on the Spirit is life and peace. For the mind that is set on the flesh is hostile to God. . . . Those who are in the flesh cannot please God." I believe that this passage can correctly be paraphrased as follows: "For those who live on the natural level think on that level, but those who live on the supernatural level think supernaturally. A natural-level mentality is death, but a supernatural, life and peace. Wherefore natural level thinking is inimical to God. . . . Those who live on the natural level cannot please God."

Sarx, as designating the purely natural level, does not thereby condemn human nature as such. Human nature — flesh — indeed can and must seek God, know what it can about him and love him: " . . . what can be known about God is plain to them [pagans], because God has shown it to them" (Rm 1:19). There is, then, a tendency in man to rise above the natural, to stretch his arms toward the supernatural, i.e., to the realm of spirit or *pneuma*. This *sarx* will not do. "So they are without excuse; for although they knew God they did not honor him as God or give thanks. . ." Rm 1:20–21). "Their conscience also bears witness and their conflicting thoughts accuse or perhaps excuse them" (Rm 2:15). For Paul those who live by the flesh are those who choose to live on the merely human level.

But, as we have seen, life on this level ends in "jealousy and quarrels" and worse, as Paul delineates in Romans 1: 26–32. Why is this? It is because the flesh is weak. First of all, it is powerless of itself to rise to God. "Those who are in the flesh cannot please God" (Rm 8:8), in the sense that they don't have the power to do so. "For I know that in me, that is, in my flesh, no good dwells, because to wish is within my power, but I do not find the strength to accomplish what is good" (Rm 7:18; Conf. tr.).

The impotence of the flesh for anything in the divine order results from its peculiar nature in man: man is not only flesh, he is also spirit (*pneuma*). An animal is only flesh, but man is not. He is "flesh" from only one aspect. As spirit he may not live as flesh alone. The latter is subordinated to the former and directed by it. "So then, brethren, we are debtors, not to the flesh [i.e., the merely human] — for if you live according to the flesh you will die, but if by the Spirit you put to death the deeds of the body, you will live" (Rm 8:12–13). We shall see this in detail in the chapter on the spirit in Paul, where we shall be better able to contrast flesh and spirit and understand their relationship.

Man as "flesh" is morally weak not merely because of his radical impotence, but also because of the sin of Adam and its effects on the human race. "Therefore as sin came into the world through one man and death through sin . . ."; "For if many died through one man's trespass . . ."; "Then one man's trespass led to condemnation for all men, so one man's act of righteousness leads to acquittal and life for all men. For as by one man's disobedience many were made sinners, so by one man's obedience many will be made righteous" (Rm 5:12, 15, 18–19).

Hence the "flesh" has lusts (Rm 13:14; Eph 2:3). Paul brings this out graphically, drawing on his own experience, in Romans 7:5–25. When the convert Christians were ruled by the flesh, "sinful passions, aroused by the law, were at work in our members to bear fruit for death" (Rm 7:5); " . . . but I see in my members another law at war with the law of my mind and making me captive to the law of sin which dwells in my members" (Rm 7:23). This struggle Paul details in the well-known passage, Galatians 5:16–26, where the basic premise is that the "flesh" lusts against the "spirit." Because of this disordered desire there result not only the so-called "sins of the flesh," but also those which are essentially intellectual: idolatry, witchcraft, enmity, jealousy, quarreling, anger, factions. Original sin has weakened the whole man, and left him prone to sin, inimical to the *pneuma*, to the spirit of God. Before baptism Christians were "the slaves of sin" (Rm 6:17, 20).

"Flesh," *sarx*, as designating fallen human nature, is the result of Adam's sin, which left human nature in this sin-prone condition. And man's further sins have strengthened this tendency. William Barclay has put this very well, and given at the same time a good definition of Paul's particular use of *sarx*: "The flesh is what man has made himself in contrast with man as God made him. The flesh is man as he has allowed himself to become in contrast with man as God meant him to be. The flesh stands for the total effect upon man of his own sin and of the sin of his fathers and of the sin of all men who have gone before him. The flesh is human nature as it has become through sin. . . . The flesh is man as he is apart from Jesus Christ and his Spirit."[21]

Of the various biblical meanings of *bashar* and *sarx* there are three which stand out as more marked, particularly with

---

[21] William Barclay, *Flesh and Spirit* (Nashville: Abingdon Press, 1962), p. 22.

reference to sarx with its New Testament development. First, it stands for the whole man, not merely the body, or "flesh" with all of its Western connotations. Man does not have sarx; he is sarx. Second, man is not sarx alone, but pneuma also, and there is a fundamental clash between the two that results not from difference in substance, but difference in orders, in orientation. Lastly, sarx is in opposition to God, because it represents not an ideal human nature, hypothetical man in the state of pure nature, but man as he existentially is and has become, thanks to himself. As Werner Kümmel has put it: "Sarx denotes the man who lets himself be determined by his actual historical existence in the world; it does not describe man in his fundamental nature, but rather in his membership in this passing evil age."[22]

---

[22] Werner Georg Kümmel, op. cit., pp. 62–63.

CHAPTER 3

Soul

From bashar we proceed to the study of man as nephesh. Gerhard von Rad writes: "The most important concept in this anthropology [i.e. biblical anthropology] is that of the nephesh."[1] We have seen in the last two chapters that bashar stands for man under the aspect of his body, his flesh, and that, because the Hebrews saw man whole, it could even depict him as thinking and willing. However, this extension of the word's meaning to include these rational activities is accidental. Basically, bashar relates man to the animal kingdom, to the earth.

The reason why nephesh is such an important concept is that it provides the differentiating characteristic: nephesh is the distinctively human element in man; it designates the existence of man as human, as a person.

NEPHESH-PSYCHĒ IN THE OLD TESTAMENT

Nephesh is regularly translated in the Septuagint by psychē, and the latter word carries over the same concepts into the New Testament. Its original meaning was "throat" or "neck," an example of which we can see in Habakkuk 2:5. From the transitional meaning of "breath" it came to convey that of animal life, and, in the Bible, chiefly human life.[2]

"Then the Lord God formed man of dust from the ground, and breathed into his nostrils the breath of life; and man

---

[1] Gerhard von Rad, *Old Testament Theology* (New York: Harper and Brothers, 1962), p. 153.

[2] Cf. Aubrey R. Johnson, *The Vitality of the Individual in the Thought of Ancient Israel* (Cardiff: The University of Wales Press, 1949), p. 9. This is a carefully prepared work, now a standard, in which the author discusses bashar, nephesh, and ruach.

became a living being" (Gn 2:7). "Living being" here translates nephesh hayyah. We find the same Hebrew expression
in Genesis 1:20, which the Confraternity version renders as
simply "life" and the RSV as "living creatures." The meaning
in either passage is "living, breathing thing," no more, no less.
Nephesh, at base, is the animating principle of animal life.[3]
It is the nephesh that gives life to the bashar, but not as a
distinct substance. Adam doesn't have nephesh; he is nephesh,
just as he is bashar. The body, far from being divided from
its animating principle, is the visible nephesh. J. Pedersen
summed up the usual Hebrew viewpoint, employing the body-
soul terminology, in what has become a commonplace:
"The body is the soul in its outward form."[4]

This viewpoint is so foreign to our Hellenistic approach
to man: the body as prison of the soul. So many of our
spiritual writers, great, and sound in other respects, have
given the impression that the disembodied soul is the Christian ideal. Trample the body, deny it everything but the bare
necessities, and free the soul! This thinking may do for a
school of some sort of spirituality, but it is hardly that of
authentic Judeo-Christianity. Man as nephesh means that it
is his nephesh that goes to dinner, that tackles a steak and
eats it. When I see another person, what I see is not merely
his body, but his visible nephesh, because in the terms of
Genesis 2:7, that is what a man is — a living nephesh. The
eyes have been called "the windows of the soul." This is
actually dichotomy. The eyes, as long as they belong to a
living person, are in themselves the revelation of the soul.

1. Nephesh as Human Life

In most of the twenty-two earliest occurrences of nephesh
the meaning is simply life.[5] For example: ". . . they seek my

---

[3] Cf. Bruce Vawter, C.M., A Path through Genesis (New York: Sheed
and Ward, 1956), p. 53.

[4] J. Pedersen, Israel: Its Life and Culture (Oxford: Oxford University Press,
1946), I–II, p. 171.

[5] Cf. Daniel Lys, Nèphèsh: Histoire de l'Ame dans la Revelation d'Israel
(Paris: Presses Universitaires de France, 1959), p. 124. I have followed the
chronology of this invaluable monograph in this chapter.

life to take it away" (1 K 19:10, 14); "Pray, let me live" (1 K 20:32); "The man who allows any of those whom I give into your hands to escape shall forfeit his life" (2 K 10:24). It is true that *nephesh* is translated *soul* in 1 Kings 17:21–22 — " 'O Lord my God, let this child's soul come into him again'; . . . and the soul of the child came into him again, and he revived" — but *nephesh* here means only the child's life, his vitality which makes him a living human being. This same basic concept conveyed by *nephesh* extends throughout the whole Old Testament, in all periods and in all types: "because . . . I love you, I give men in return for you, peoples in exchange for your life" (Is 43:4); " . . . then he shall die for his sin, but you shall save your life" (Ezk 3:19); " . . . give me my life for which I ask . . ." (Est 7:3); "He who guards his way preserves his life" (Pr 16:17).[6]

But *nephesh* can also mean the life of non-rational animals. This is seen, for example, in two passages which explain the Hebrews' veneration of blood: " . . . for the blood is the life, and you shall not eat the life with the flesh" (Dt 12:23); "For the life of the flesh is in the blood; and I have given it for you upon the altar to make atonement for your souls; for it is the blood that makes atonement, by reason of the life" (Lv 17:11). This latter passage refers to the sacrificial procedure of pouring the drained blood of the animal at the base or on the sides of the altar; the first, to eating flesh-meat. The thing to note is that each *life* in these texts translates *nephesh*, and that, therefore, both blood and *nephesh* are common to men and animals. In the Leviticus text *nephesh* means not only "the life of the flesh," but also "your souls," human life, that is, as well as animal.[7] Hence, we can say that *nephesh* is the animating principle of all animal life.

But the Bible is concerned with men, not animals, so *nephesh* basically designates human beings as alive. Because it is, then, the animating principle of human life, it is a

---

[6] Cf. Gn 2:6; 19:17; 32:31; Ex 21:23; 1 S 18:3; 2 K 4:2; Pss 31:14; 94:21; Pr 6:26; 16:17; 22:5; 29:10; Je 4:10; 5:9; 20:13; Ezk 18:27.

[7] Cf. Gn 1:20–21, 24, 30; 9:10, 12, 15, 16; Lv 17:14; 24:17; Jb 12:20; BS 16:28, 31.

logical center of emotional activity.[8] We see this nuance expressed in one of the earliest uses of the word: in 2 Kings 4:27 the nephesh of the Shunammitess is in anguish. "This is to say," comments Lys, "that it is the seat of sadness, hence of the emotions and sentiments, of the affective, and not simply of the vegetative, life."[9] So the nephesh feels sorrow: "all the people were bitter in soul [nephesh], each for his sons and daughters. . . " (1 S 30:6). And bitterness: "Another dies in bitterness of soul [nephesh], never having tasted of good" (Jb 21:25).[10] But the emotion which nephesh more often expresses is desire. We find expressions such as "the desire of your nephesh," "as your nephesh desires" (Cf. Dt 12:20; 14:26; 1 S 2:16; 2 S 3:21; Is 26:8). Desire in the Old Testament is chiefly the function of the nephesh, possibly because it is the life-principle. The instinct of self-preservation sets up a series of desires aimed at the maintenance of life, often of life on a wider scale than mere survival. It is not strange therefore to find nephesh — and its Septuagint equivalent psychē — designating disordered desire. This is illustrated in the Greek book of Sirach: " . . . burning passion is a blazing fire, not to be quenched till it burns itself out" (BS 23:16). The Greek for "burning passion" is literally a "hot psychē." We are a long way here from the soul-body dichotomy of Platonism, and much nearer to present-day psychosomatic medicine and depth psychology.

It is natural that this principle also thinks, wills, loves, and is at the root of what have come to be known as "psychical" activities. However, we must beware of jumping to conclusions here and rashly presuming that these usages prove the existence of the soul as we know it. If we did we would be embarrassed to discover that the heart, leb, lebab, is used 204 times to express intellectual activities, and 190 times to denote volitional activities, a good deal more often than

---

8 The nephesh is only one center of the emotions because, as we have already seen in the two previous chapters, the bashar, and especially the heart, bowels, and other parts of the body are also such centers.

9 Daniel Lys, op. cit., p. 126.

10 The Confraternity-Douay version has soul in these two passages.

nephesh is used to express the same.[11] It is important to note, however, that the nephesh thinks, understands, and wills. "It is not good for a man [nephesh] to be without knowledge . . . ," (Pr 19:2); "there is no knowledge of the nephesh, there is no good . . ." "Your understanding [psychē] covered the whole earth . . ." (BS 47:15); "thou dost not give him up to the will [nephesh] of his enemies" (Ps 41:2). The bride of the Song of Songs demands: "Tell me, you whom my soul [nephesh] loves . . ." (1:7). Love, while essentially an activity of the will, has other facets and makes use of other human elements. We see this in the passage referring to the friendship of David and Jonathan: " . . . the soul of Jonathan was knit to the soul of David, and Jonathan loved him as his own soul" (1 S 18:1). Each "soul" here translates nephesh. While the last means life, or even the person of Jonathan, the first two embrace the whole complex of the act and fact of friendship: the good in the other that is lovable, the "kindredness," the choosing of and going out to the other, the union of wills that is the substance of love.[12]

Further, the nephesh "thirsts for God" (Pss 42:3; 63:2), yearns for him (Is 26:9), lives to praise him (Ps 119:175). We must search for him with the whole heart and the whole nephesh (Dt 4:29). Thus the nephesh is capable not only of psychical activities, but also of directing these to God.

The parallel use of heart and nephesh in Deuteronomy 4:29 may be disquieting, especially since we have already learned the importance of the heart as the chief center of intellect and will.[13] And when we see from its use that the heart was considered as a seat of the emotions, and represented the very character and interior dispositions of a person, we ask whether, principle of life notwithstanding, the Hebrews didn't regard the heart, rather than the nephesh, as the center of a man.

But this could hardly be the case, because the Hebrews regarded man as a "living being [nephesh]" (Gn 2:7), as we saw

---

[11] The tabulation is Robinson's in The Christian Doctrine of Man, p. 22.
[12] Cf. Ps 26:12; 1 Par 28:9; BS 37:12; 51:24; Ws 7:27; 9:15; 10:16.
[13] The Hebrews so regarded it. Cf. Robinson, op. cit., p. 26.

above, not as a living heart, or *bashar*. Their concept of man was fundamentally as being a *nephesh*, or soul. "Such as he is," Pedersen wrote, "man, in his total essence, is a soul."[14] This is the reason why *nephesh*, with a suffix, in 70 instances means simply the personal pronoun, and in 53, the reflexive pronoun. The *nephesh* is the person.[15]

Before we study the *nephesh* as person, one other aspect of the term with regard to human nature must be considered. There are a number of texts which depict the *nephesh* as the seat of the appetite. The hungry or empty "soul" is mentioned in Psalm 107:9; Numbers 11:6; Isaiah 29:8; 32:6. In Proverbs 25:25 we read: "Like cold water to a thirsty soul. . . ." Hunger and thirst come about because of life which depends on food and drink for its existence. "Hungry and thirsty, their soul [*nephesh*] fainted within them" (Ps 107:5). It is noteworthy that "soul" here does not hunger after some intellectual object, truth, for instance, but after food. *Nephesh* in these passages means simply that animating principle that creates the animal appetite.[16]

These texts remind us that the Hebrews saw man as a whole. The thirsty soul drinking the cold water is actually the mouth, throat, and other parts of the digestive system *in action*. It is the activity of the body caused by hunger and thirst, as well as by the satisfaction of these appetites, that the Hebrews could call *nephesh*. Again, *nephesh* includes the flesh as alive. And, as I have just said, life and action produce these natural appetites.

2. Nephesh as Person

The Hebrews saw the *nephesh* as the seat of the personality. To refer to the *nephesh* was to refer to what we would call the person, the individual, to human nature as responsible.

---

14 Pedersen, op. cit., p. 99.

15 For example: Nm 30:5, "her *nephesh*" is herself; Ex 31:14, "his *nephesh*," he; Ps 33:3, "my *nephesh*," I; Lv 27:2, "his *nephesh*," himself, etc. As to heart, Pedersen wrote: "Where special emphasis is put on the tendency of the soul [the will], the word heart is often used" (op. cit., p. 103). The heart, then, is the soul, the *nephesh*, but under certain aspects [ibid., p. 104].

16 It is also the *nephesh* which is filled: cf. Pr 13:25; 27:7; Ec 6:7.

At once we see the great difference between it and *bashar*. The latter is human nature, and may stand for the whole man, but only in his solidarity with humanity and it emphasizes man's weakness and instability. *Nephesh* stands for this human nature as a responsible person.

In one of the earliest texts we find the expression, "As the Lord lives, and as you yourself live" (2 K 2:2, 4, 6). "You yourself" translates *nephesh*. The reason for this is obvious: *nephesh* parallels "the Lord." *Yahweh* in the Hebrew text means not only God's life, his vitality as such, but his whole being; hence, *nephesh* here means the person, Elijah in this case, in the totality of his being. We find the expression in another very early text (2 K 4:30, also in 1 S 25:26 [J]); in a later but still pre-Amos passage, "As your soul lives" (1 S 17:55) can be taken to mean, "As you live," because of the earlier parallelism. *Nephesh* is the individual in six verses of Joshua 10 (JE). For example: "[They] smote it [Hebron] with the edge of the sword, and its kings and its towns, and every person [*nephesh*] in it" (v. 37; cf. vv. 28, 30, 32, 35, 39). It is noteworthy especially in view of the idea of the *nephesh* as separable from the *bashar* after death, that *nephesh* in these earliest texts could mean more than its basic concept of life, and could be extended to embrace the composite concept of the living person.

Because of this extension Amos could write: "The Lord God has sworn by his very *nephesh*" (6:8), translated by the Revised Standard Version as "himself." Here there is no question of an anthropomorphism, of the application to God of one of the narrower meanings of *nephesh*, even of "soul," as the Douay version reads. God, insofar as he is personal and individual, is seen simply as a *nephesh*.

This use of *nephesh* with regard to man continues through the later books.[17] But there is a developed meaning, related to and dependent upon *person*, which we must consider. In Micah we read: "Shall I give my first-born for my crime, the

---

[17] Cf. Is 3:9; Je 26:19; 38:17, 20; 43:6; Ezk 18:4, 20, 27; Gn 23:8; Est 4:13; 9:31; Nm 19:18; 1 Mc 10:33. This list is incomplete.

fruit of my body for the sin of my soul [nephesh]?" (6:7.)
The parallelism is: first-born — crime; fruit of my body —
sin of my nephesh. The meaning in either part of the verse is
the same; the second part is simply an embellishment of the
first. The Hebrew word translated here by "body" is beten,
which means belly, or womb; hence there is no question of opposing body and soul. The meaning is not that the soul is the
human cause of sin, with the body as the soul's instrument.
Rather, the nephesh, the whole living person, is the cause
of sin. Therefore, in this verse, responsibility for sin is attributed to the nephesh as the person.

We find the same idea in a number of texts which treat
of sin and guilt: "If any one [nephesh] sins unwittingly . . ."
(Lv 4:2); "If any one [nephesh] sins in that he hears a public
adjuration to testify and though he is a witness . . . yet does
not speak, he shall bear his iniquity" (Lv 5:1); "But the
person [nephesh] who does anything with a high hand,
whether he is native or a sojourner, reviles the Lord, and
. . . shall be cut off from among his people" (Nm 15:30);
"Behold, all souls [nephashoth] are mine . . . the soul
[nephesh] that sins shall die" (Ezk 18:4).[18] The nephesh
as the responsible person is a simple conclusion from the
basic concept: the nephesh in enlivening the bashar gives
it existence as such — as a human being, and as an individual
human being. As the living person, the nephesh is this particular human being who is the agent of his own actions, who
thinks, wills, and is answerable for his conduct, that is, a
responsible person.

In other words, where there's life, there's nephesh. Any
activity, psychical, physical, or psychophysical, was done by
the nephesh because such activity presumed and manifested
life. The whole nephesh was involved in eating, walking, thirst-
ing, loving, thinking. The Hebrew did not divide and assign
human activities. Any act was the whole nephesh in action,
hence, the whole person. As W. D. Stacey so well puts it:
"Nephesh sorrowed, hungered and thought because each

---

18 Cf. Lv 5:2, 4, 15, 17, 21; Nm 5:6; 15:27, 28; 31:28.

of these functions required the whole personality to perform it, and the distinction between emotional, physical, and mental was not made."[19]

To say that the *nephesh* is the person is not to say that the soul is the person. The *nephesh* includes and presumes the *bashar*. In fact, the ancient Hebrews could not possibly conceive of one without the other. Here was no Greek dichotomy of soul and body, of two opposing substances, but a unity, man, who is *bashar* from one aspect and *nephesh* from another. *Bashar*, then, is the *concrete reality* of human existence, *nephesh* is the *personality* of human existence.

But we can still conclude that in some way the Hebrews regarded the *nephesh* as the seat of the personality. I say "in some way" because they did not think along these lines. They had little use for abstractions, and none for clear-cut distinctions with regard to man. As for us, I think that we must come to the same conclusion: "in some way" the *nephesh* is the center of the personality, for it is the individual as active in every human activity, the person, therefore, as responsible.

The idea of the *nephesh* as the responsible person is best grasped from the Hebrew's beliefs concerning life after death. It is not my purpose here to explore these beliefs in detail and to argue that some books of the Old Testament accepted the survival of the *nephesh* after death, but in my concern to present the "personal" character of the *nephesh* I must at least sketch the development of belief in a personal survival and, therefore, of a separable *nephesh*.[20]

The Jews of Old Testament times were forced to accept the fact of the person's survival after death. Forced, because only a belief in the resurrection of the body, which belief came with time and apocalyptists, could explain the existence of the *nephesh* as an entity apart. The notion of life after death

---

[19] W. David Stacey, *The Pauline View of Man* (London: Macmillan and Co., Ltd., 1956), p. 87.

[20] R. H. Charles has a lengthy treatment of the Hebrews' beliefs about life after death in his *Eschatology* (New York: Schocken Books, 1963). This is a paperback reprint of an old work which is not without its weaknesses.

developed slowly, because life meant *nephesh* and *bashar* to-gether, and if the *nephesh* is to survive without the *bashar* it could hardly be said to live. "The dead is a soul [sic] bereft of strength," wrote Pedersen.

> "The dead is still a soul, but a soul that has lost its substance and strength: it is as a misty vapour or a shadow. Even after death the soul still maintains its intimate relation with the body. The dead body is still the soul. . . . As long as the body is a body, the soul is closely connected with it."[21]

This is the reason why the dead body could be called a *nephesh*: "If one who is unclean from contact with a dead body [*nephesh*] . . ." (Hag 2:13); "None of them shall de-file himself for the dead [*nephesh*] among his people . . ." (Lv 21:1); "All the days that he separates himself to the Lord, he shall not go near a dead body [*nephesh*]" (Nm 6:6).

The underlying idea of *nephesh*, in these and similar texts, whether the literal expression is an unclean *nephesh*, or that of a dead man, is that this corpse is still the person. *Nephesh* here can no longer mean the animating principle; this is ob-vious. But it still connotes the seat of the personality. Granted the existence of the body, dead though it be, it is the *nephesh*, too, as in life, because the Jew was unable to separate the two. But now the *nephesh* is only the person. The *nephesh* stays with the body, perhaps as long as it is recognizable, which is a logical conclusion from the Hebrew concept.

But then what? Here we must consider the gloomy notion of Sheol. Sheol was the abode of the dead, an ancient notion common to inhabitants of the Tigris and Euphrates Valley in the time of Abraham. There is nothing religious about the notion. In fact, the earliest view of it was of a place removed from Yahweh's control, where all relations with him were broken: "For in death there is no remembrance of thee; in Sheol who can give thee praise?" (Ps 6:5.) With the proph-ets' revelation of Yahweh as the one and only God, rather than as the tribal god of Israel, the Hebrews realized that

---

[21] J. Pedersen, *op. cit.*, p. 180.

his power extended even to Sheol: "Though they dig into Sheol, from there shall my hand take them . . ." (Am 9:2); "If I ascend to heaven, thou art there! if I make my bed in Sheol, thou art there" (Ps 139:8).

Originally Sheol was conceived as the abode of all the dead, good and bad. But Job expresses a hope, a wish is more like it, in some kind of release from it after a time (14:13–15). The author of Psalm 49 voices a definite conviction: "But God will ransom my soul from the power of Sheol, for he will receive me" (v. 15), although the wicked have to remain there. And the same conviction occurs in a beautiful passage of Psalm 73: "Nevertheless I am continually with thee; thou dost hold my right hand. Thou dost guide me with thy counsel, and afterward thou wilt receive me to glory. . . . My flesh and my heart may fail, but God is the strength of my heart and my portion for ever" (vv. 23–24, 26). The faithful Israelite came to believe that his life of union with Yahweh could not possibly end with a bleak existence in Sheol.

Sheol thus came to be considered a temporary abode for the just, a waiting place, while for the wicked — "Sheol shall be their home" (Ps 49:14). However, Daniel taught an actual resurrection for some: the dead heroes and saints of Israel, those who contributed to its world-rule, would rise to glory, and those Israelites who were its enemies would rise to shame and punishment (Dn 12:2–3). Along with this doctrine was that contained in the apocryphal book, 1 Enoch. Actually this book is a compilation, dating probably from about 160 to 60 B.C.[22] Because of different authors and times of composition there seems to be an inconsistency in doctrine here, but what really happened was a progression: from a belief in a resurrection of the just for a certain time (1 Enoch 25), there developed a belief in a resurrection for eternity (1 Enoch 90). The abode of the risen, too, progressed from a renovated but still earthly Jerusalem to a heavenly Jerusa-

---

[22] Cf. Artur Weiser, *Introduction to the Old Testament* (London: Darton, Longman and Todd, 1961), pp. 427–428; D. S. Russell, *Between the Testaments* (Philadelphia: Muhlenberg Press, 1960), p. 85.

lem.[23] We find the belief in a resurrection in another work of the same period, the Testament of the Twelve Patriarchs (Test. Benj. 10:6–8). Thus when Martha says to Christ concerning Lazarus: "I know that he will rise at the resurrection, on the last day" (Jn 11:24), she is simply voicing a belief common at that time. When Christ tells the Jews: "Do not marvel at this; for the hour is coming when all who are in the tombs will hear his [the Son of Man's] voice and come forth, those who have done good, to the resurrection of life, and those who have done evil, to the resurrection of judgment" (Jn 5:28–29), the only new thing he tells them is that *he* is the Son of Man.

Belief in a resurrection was widespread by the time of Christ. Described more fully by the popular apocryphal works, it was, nevertheless, the logical outcome of the basic, intimate, relationship between Yahweh and his people, of the underlying Father-Son relationship between God and Israel. Resurrection, apart from a direct revelation in the Old Testament, would be anyway a valid theological conclusion drawn from biblical fundamentals. When the writer of 1 Enoch 22 describes the three divisions of Sheol, he is building on what has already been believed. Life after death, immediate reward and punishment, even before resurrection, can hardly come as novelties in the second century B.C. And when Christ tells the good thief: "Truly, I say to you, today you will be with me in paradise" (Lk 23:43), he presumes a long and firm tradition of *biblical* faith and hope.

I hope that this sketchy account, which may seem to be a digression but actually is necessary, has at least indicated that the Hebrews definitely believed in a life after death. The question now to be considered is, what survived? As we have seen, it had to be the person, but the Hebrews could not call it the *nephesh*, because of the complete unity of man which demanded that flesh, *bashar*, accompany *nephesh* or soul. The *nephesh* remained with the *bashar* until its disso-

---

[23] Cf. R. H. Charles, *op. cit.*, pp. 219–220, 223. Cf. also the same author's monumental *The Apocrypha and Pseudepigrapha of the Old Testament* (Oxford: Clarendon Press, 1913), vol. II.

lution; then, as I said above, the person went to Sheol. Since the Hebrews could not possibly conceive of the nephesh living apart from the bashar, they referred to dead persons as the rephaīm, which is generally translated by "shades," i.e., ghosts.[24] These were wraiths of the former individuals, barely substantial ghosts, wandering in Sheol, devoid of vitality: "Sheol is all astir preparing for your coming; it awakens the rephaīm to greet you, all the leaders of the earth. . . . All of them speak out and say to you, 'You too have become weak like us, you are the same as we' " (Is 14:9–10; my translation). Hence, Sheol cannot be considered to be a place of life, but more one of existence. This is another reason why the Hebrews could not see the nephesh in Sheol, for it is the life-principle of a man.

Nevertheless, it was the nephesh that was in Sheol, even if the Hebrews did not use the term, because as the seat of the personality, its bearer, only man as nephesh, could survive when the bashar was no more. The Hebrews called their dead rephaīm, but they meant the person. In all references to the dead as in some way alive, it is understood that the person is meant, and not some vestigial phantom of the human being. He may not have his body, and his vitality may be low, but it is he, or what's left of him.

The dead person was not completely "spiritual," or incorporal, but had a ghostly body, since the nephesh could not exist entirely apart from the bashar, and thus was recognizable if he had to make an earthly appearance. Our popular notion of ghosts is absolutely Hebraic as to the true physical nature of the rephaīm. For example, when the witch of Endor "brings up" Samuel from Sheol, he is recognizable even from his prophet's outergarment, the melōtes (1 S 28:11–14); Israel's enemies are recognizable in Sheol from the fact of their uncircumcision (Ezk 32:21, 24, 26, 28–30, 32).[25]

The rephaīm were not so devoid of life that they could not know what was going on on earth. Rachel mourns be-

---

[24] Cf. Jb 26:5; Ps 88:11; Pr 2:18; 9:18; 21:16; Is 26:14, 19.
[25] Cf 1 K 2:6; Is 14:9, 15–16.

cause her children have left her tomb and gone into exile
(Je 31:15). And Samuel, in the incident referred to above,
is quite aware of what Saul has been doing. The practice of
consulting mediums, although they may be fraudulent, attests
to the belief in the knowledge and interest of the dead (Lv
19:31; 20:6; Is 8:19; 19:3).[26]

In other words, what was in Sheol was the person, capable
in some limited way of personal acts proper to him, with the
individual as their agent. When the author of Psalm 16 wrote:
"For thou dost not give me [i.e., my nephesh] up to Sheol..."
(v. 10), he was expressing what had been believed all along,
that it was the person, the nephesh, that was in Sheol. One
of the earliest texts of the Bible, 1 Kings 17:21–22, conceives of the nephesh as able to leave the body and return
again.[27] In view of all the facts, it can be said that the Hebrews believed the nephesh could and did exist after death,
separated from the bashar insofar as the latter was the body.
But still it could not exist totally separated, for it had a bodily
form and some extremely slight substance. And it was bashar
in its complete humanness, with human concerns, even emotions. It was indeed not the freed, disembodied soul of Plato.

Therefore, when the author of Wisdom wrote of the
psychē, he was not writing of the Platonic soul, but of the
psychē which in the Septuagint translates nephesh. There
is no reason to understand the following passage in a Platonic
and not biblical sense: "But the souls [psychai] of the righteous are in the hand of God, and no torment will ever touch
them. In the eyes of the foolish they seemed to have died,
and their departure was thought to be an affliction, and their
going from us to be their destruction; but they are at peace"
(3:1–3). Some commentators feel that the author teaches
a definite dichotomy of soul and body (cf. 9:15; 16:14),

---

[26] For an opposite view cf. Ec 9:5; 12:7; Pss 104:29–30; 146:4, although
except for the first passage, perhaps, the others could admit of a more opti-
mistic interpretation.

[27] Cf. Daniel Lys, op. cit., p. 126. For this interpretation of Ps 16:10,
cf. Artur Weiser, The Psalms (Philadelphia: The Westminster Press, 1962),
pp. 176–178. For a text parallel to 1 K 17:21–22, cf. 2 K 4:34 ff.

influenced by the Platonic philosophy of Alexandria, where he wrote. But Edmund Hill thinks not: "Nonetheless the whole context and approach and flavour of his thought is Hebrew through and through." However, he adds: "His phrase 'the souls of the just' [3:1] would be equally well, perhaps better translated 'the lives of the just.' "²⁸ Because the author *is* Hebrew through and through, because of the whole meaning of *nephesh-psychē*, and because of the Hebrews' beliefs concerning life after death, we are justified in translating *psychai* here as "souls," understanding "persons" and the whole context of meanings contained in the word *nephesh*.²⁹

As to the Platonic sounding "For a perishable body [*sōma*] weighs down the soul [*psychē*] . . ." (9:15), there is no reason to believe that the author departs from the usual Hebrew concept of man. The expression may be Greek, but the thought is Hebrew.

The Jews did not speculate as to the nature of man, his composition. They took him as he appeared to be — living, apparent to the senses, and oriented to God — and let it go at that. The Greeks were the curious ones as to just what *is* man, but not the Jews. Hence it was not the *nephesh* alone that was immortal, but the *nephesh* as the person, somehow including the body because the Jews could not conceive of

---

²⁸ Edmund Hill, " 'Soul' in the Bible," *Life of the Spirit*, vol. XIII, No. 156 (June, 1959), p. 536.

²⁹ By the time of the author of Wisdom the idea of the detached *nephesh-psychē* seems to have been fairly common and accepted by the Hebrews, as we can see in the apocrypha. E.g.: "And grieve not if your soul [*psychē*] into Sheol has descended in grief . . ." (1 Enoch 102:5, p. 274). Cf. also 1 Enoch 9:10, p. 193; 22:3-4, p. 202; 102:4-5, pp. 273-274; 103:7, p. 275). The *nephesh* of the dead becomes "spirit," *pneuma*, in Bar 2:17 and Tb 3:6, and we find that the dead are referred to as "spirits" in the apocrypha and the Dead Sea Scrolls, but this was due to the fact that by this time *ruach-pneuma* was a popular, although not exact, synonym for *nephesh-psychē* and has the acquired meaning of the Hebrew "soul." Cf. 1 Enoch 22:5-7, 9, 11-13, pp. 202-203; 98:10, p. 269; 103:3-4, 8, pp. 274-275 (although "souls" occurs in v. 7); Jubilees 23:31, p. 49. The page numbers refer to R. H. Charles, *The Apocrypha and Pseudepigrapha of the Old Testament*. 1 Enoch has the interesting expression "spirits of the souls of the dead," 1 Enoch 22:3-4, p. 202. For the Dead Sea Scrolls cf. J. Van Der Ploeg, O.P., *Le Rouleau de la Guerre* (Leiden: E. J. Brill, 1959), p. 42; Menahem Mansoor, *The Thanksgiving Hymns* (Leiden: E. J. Brill, 1961), pp. 151-152.

one without the other. We can look at the immortality of the whole man from the standpoint of the covenant. A passage in Deuteronomy (30:15–20) speaks of life as the result of keeping the covenant: "Therefore choose life, that you and your descendants may live, loving the Lord your God, obeying his voice, and cleaving to him; for that means life to you and length of days, that you may dwell in the land which the Lord swore to your fathers, to Abraham, to Isaac, and to Jacob, to give them" (vv. 19–20). But the principle of human life — the life of the whole person — is the *nephesh*. Just as a man, a *nephesh* therefore, who keeps the covenant could hope for a long life on the land of Israel, so also could he hope for a continued prolongation after death of that life with God, as we have seen. And that life was in the *nephesh*.

I conclude this section of the chapter with an observation that by now should be superfluous, namely, that the Old Testament texts make it quite clear that the *nephesh* indicates *natural* man, just as does *bashar*. As principle of life, as the personal principle of a human being, *nephesh* is as earthbound and horizontal as *bashar*. The fact that it is immortal, capable of living with God, adds nothing to the stature of the concept. It means simply that *this person* can live eternally. The capability for living with God is rather because of spirit (*ruach*).

Psychē in the New Testament

Psychē, the New Testament (and Septuagint) translation of *nephesh*, has its same meanings. *Psychē* expresses the vitality, the animating principle of human nature, true, but especially the personality, the responsible agent of human action. In many instances in the New Testament — as in the Old — *psychē* can best be translated by "self," including the pejorative connotations of that word that "selfishness" and "self-centered" conjure up in our minds. The French *moi* is correct here, too, as well as "Ego" (without all of the Freudian overtones).

We understand simple vitality, that which is maintained

by food, in this passage: "Therefore I tell you, do not be anxious about your life [*psychē*], what you shall eat. . . . For life [*psychē*] is more than food . . ." (Lk 12:22–23).[30] The *psychē* is the animating principle: "Is it lawful on the Sabbath . . . to save life [*psychē*], or to kill?" (Mk 3:4); "The good shepherd lays down his life [*psychē*] for his sheep" (Jn 10:11); " . . . for he nearly died for the work of Christ, risking his life [*psychē*] to complete your service to me" (Phil 2:30).[31]

As in the Old Testament, so in the New Testament man is a living *psychē*. Therefore emotions are attributed to it: "My soul [*psychē*] is very sorrowful, even to death" (Mt 26:38); "And a sword will pierce through your own soul [*psychē*] also" (Lk 2:35).[32] The *psychē* is also able to think: "But the disbelieving Jews stirred up the Gentiles and poisoned their minds [*psychas*] against the brethren" (Acts 14:2); "Since we have heard that some persons from us have troubled you with words, unsettling your minds [*psychas*]" (Acts 15:24). Volitional activity is also assigned to the *psychē*: "Whatever your task, work heartily [lit. 'from the *psychē*'], as serving the Lord and not men" (Col 3:23); " . . . doing the will of God from the heart [*psychē*]" (Eph 6:6).

However, it is *psychē* as designating the whole human person that most interests us, because this is its most essential meaning in the Bible, as well as that which distinguishes it from the Greek concept of the soul. If I have labored this point overmuch in this chapter it is only to liberate those of us who were taught about the soul solely from the standpoint of Greek philosophy, with the inevitably resultant soul-body dichotomy. When we can view, with the biblical writers — and with Christ — the soul as the *nephesh-psychē*, which is the person as living, and the body as one aspect of the *bashar-sarx*, the person as perceptible, we are more apt to have a healthier attitude toward the human person, and, indeed, toward matter in general. We will be "liberated," not by

---

[30] Cf. Mt 6:25.
[31] Cf. Mt 2:20; 20:28; Mk 10:45; Lk 6:9; Jn 13:37–38; 15:13; Rm 16:4; Js 5:20.
[32] Cf. Mt 22:37; Mk 14:34; Jn 12:27; Acts 2:43.

secularization, but by God's word. And the fact of our own personal resurrection will become a necessity.

The belief that the *psyche* is separable from the *sarx* after death and lives on in a place of reward or punishment was widely held by the time of Christ.[33] We can gather this from Christ's words in Matthew 10:28 and the parallel passage, Luke 12:4–5. His story of the rich man and the beggar Lazarus after their deaths is typically Hebrew of the period (Lk 16:22–24). First, each is consigned to a place of reward or punishment — a common belief by that time — and then each is portrayed as a person, moreover, with a body. The whole story is in the tradition of the *nephesh;* the two characters are by no means *rephaïm.* Separated *psychai* of the dead are explicitly mentioned in Revelation: " . . . I saw under the altar the souls [*psychas*] of those who had been slain for the word of God, and for the witness that they had borne" (6:9); "And I saw the souls [*psychas*] of those who had been beheaded because of their testimony to Jesus and for the word of God . . ." (20:4).[34] Here, too, the souls in question are hardly those separated entities of Greek philosophy but have voices and wear white robes. We can conclude from these texts, and from the convinced attitudes which they presume, that the *psyche* after death was considered to be the person, and though separated from the *sarx-soma*, it was still so related to it as to be portrayed as having some kind of body.

Psyche is used for the whole living person: "Let every person [*pasa psyche*] be subject to the governing authorities . . ." (Rm 13:1); "We were in all two hundred and seventy-six persons [*psychai*] in the ship" (Acts 27:37); "Now I call God to witness against me [my *psyche*] . . ." (2 Co 1:23). In the last passage "myself" would be the best translation. *Psychai* is translated as "souls" in 1 Peter 1:9: " . . . the salvation of your souls," but by now we understand the whole man, and the expression should read, "the salvation of your-

---

[33] Cf. Joseph Bonsirven, S.J., *Palestinian Judaism in the Time of Jesus Christ* (New York: Holt, Rinehart and Winston, 1964), pp. 163–164.
[34] Cf. Acts 2:27, 31.

selves," or simply, "your salvation."[35] The *psychē* is the person as the responsible agent of his own conduct: "There will be tribulation and distress for every human being [*psychē*] who does evil, for Jew first and then for Greek" (Rm 2:9).

There are many texts which give a wider and deeper meaning to *psychē*. Take, for example, this text: " . . . men who have risked their lives [*psychas*] for the sake of our Lord Jesus Christ" (Acts 15:26). The RSV and Confraternity translation, "lives," expresses the right concept: the apostles and their associates have given Christ their persons, their whole selves, with all of their energy and endeavor. Implied is the idea of total dedication, and the power of self-determination. The individual has freely given his life to and for Christ. All of this is understood of *psychē* in this particular context.

Basically the same idea is contained in this passage and its parallels: "If any man would come after me, let him deny himself and take up his cross and follow me. For whoever would save his life [*psychē*] will lose it; and whoever loses his life [*psychē*] for my sake and the gospel's will save it. For what does it profit a man, to gain the whole world and forfeit his life [*psychē*]? For what can a man give in return for his life [*psychē*]?" (Mk 8:34–37).[36] *Psychē* here means both "life" and "self." The full meaning is best conveyed by a paraphrase: For he who would selfishly keep his life for himself will fail himself as a human being; but he who freely surrenders it to me for my purposes, will fulfill himself. *Psychē*, then, is the individual person, with all that he means when he says "me," — the self-seeking, self-interest, the willing that which pertains to and makes for his own good and welfare. "Losing his *psychē*" means more than a soul being damned to eternal suffering. Rather, it means the whole man, body and soul, missing the whole reason for his existence. It is not so much loss as failure to achieve and be fulfilled. What this fulfillment is we know: surrender of self to Christ. Man as man is destined to be "in Christ" (the Pauline ex-

---

[35] Cf. Lk 12:19; Acts 2:41; 3:23; 7:14; 2 Co 12:15; 1 Pt 1:22; 2:25; 3:20; 4:19; 2 Pt 2:14; Js 1:21.

[36] Cf. Mt 10:39; 16:25–26; Lk 9:23–24; 14:26; 17:33.

pression), that is, a part of the whole Christ, his body. This entails the relinquishing of a "me first" attitude and procedure. Because he is *psychē* a man is able to determine and decide what will develop himself. The gospel message tells him the true nature of his development: "Truly, truly, I say to you, unless a grain of wheat falls into the earth and dies, it remains alone; but if it dies, it bears much fruit. He who loves his life [*psychē*] loses it, and he who hates his life [*psychē*] in this world will keep it for eternal life" (Jn 12:24-25).[37]

Psychē indicates man as man; hence, it refers to him strictly as he is as a created, natural being. This is especially brought out by the adjective *psychikos*, which, in Paul, James, and Jude, means natural, on the natural level. Paul emphasizes this meaning by contrasting it with *pneumatikos*, the spiritual or supernatural. I think the best illustration of the basic meaning of *psychikos* is in 1 Corinthians 15:42-49. For example: "The body sown is natural [*psychikon*]; the body raised is glorified [*pneumatikon*]" (Lilly translation). Adam is the author of our purely human or natural life, so Paul calls him a *psychē*, quoting Genesis 2:7. Christ, however, the author of our supernatural life, is a *pneuma*. In the New Testament texts, as in the Old, *psychē* designates man as natural, because the *psychē* is man living as man.[38]

Both *bashar-sarx* and *nephesh-psychē* indicate natural man — man as a living person concretely situated in the world. *Bashar* adds the note of opposition to God, of man as not only prone to sin but also as the product of sin. However, this is not the complete biblical picture of man, for he is also *ruach-pneuma*, which is his radical orientation to God. Before we can consider this dimension of man, we must first study the meaning of the *ruach* of God, for the Bible uses the term in reference to God as well as to man, and often in a way that seems confusing. Instead of being confusing, I think that we shall see that such usage is actually astounding, to the full realization of the real nature of man.

---

[37] Cf. Lk 2:19; 12:16–21; Heb 10:39; 1 Pt 2:11.
[38] Cf. 1 Co 2:14; Js 3:15; Jd 19.

CHAPTER 4

The Spirit of God
in the Old Testament

We have seen what man is naturally — bashar and nephesh.
However, man is also ruach, and this fact is our principal
concern. I present in these chapters on the ruach-pneuma
— truly the heart of the book — the biblical meaning of the
term, while exploring its meaning for man, more particularly
the man of today. The Greek concept of man as body and
soul is correct as far as it goes, but it is incomplete. Man
may be body and soul as a natural person, but he is not merely
a natural person. He is completed, fulfilled, as a person by
his supernatural end, and directing him to this end, equipping
him, as it were, for it, is the spirit, the ruach.

But the Bible applies ruach both to God and to man — it
speaks of the spirit of God and the spirit of man (in fact,
at times, as in Paul, for example, there is some confusion as
to which one the writer means). We can understand the
biblical concept of man's spirit only by understanding the
biblical meaning of God's spirit. In fact, in view of the New
Testament fullness of revelation, as we shall see, man has
meaning only in relation to that Spirit who is a divine Person.
Therefore, we shall first take up the relation of ruach to God.

The original meaning of ruach was breath. From here it
was an easy transition to wind, which the ancient Hebrews
were quick to recognize as the breath of God. Another word
for breath is neshamah, which is used in Genesis 2:7, but
it occurs in the Old Testament only twenty-four times.[1]

---

[1] According to H. Wheeler Robinson's tabulation. Cf. The Christian Doctrine of Man (Edinburgh: T. and T. Clark, 1947), p. 15.

I think that, considering all the meanings of the term in the Old Testament, we can say that the ruach of God stands for God's dynamic presence. In the texts the phrase expresses either his activity in creation, or his own inner life. The Hebrews, far from seeing God as breath or wind, found that these concepts best expressed God as he revealed himself to them.

THE SPIRIT OF GOD AS POWER

God first revealed himself in creation, and here his activity was that of power. "No immanent, divine forces of nature exist. By contrast with the neighbouring religions, [for the Hebrews] nature has no power in it, no God in it."[2] Nature is "waste and void" of itself. Hence in the creation account the priestly writer visualized the ruach, the powerful breath of Yahweh, hovering over the emptiness, about to act (Gn 1:2). I shall return to the ruach as creative, but let us first see it in its meaning of wind, as power revealing the power of God. This, understandably enough, is one of the earliest biblical meanings of the word.

The wind was an important element in the life of the Near East, and especially dreaded was the east wind as an agent of calamity. The Jews in Egypt knew that " . . . the Lord brought an east wind upon the land all that day and all that night," that brought in swarms of locusts. They also knew that " . . . the Lord turned a very strong west wind, which lifted the locusts and drove them into the Red Sea" (Ex 10:13, 19). These same Jews witnessed the fact that " . . . the Lord drove the sea back with a strong east wind all night, and made the sea dry land" (Ex 14:21). Early in Jewish history the people associated the wind with God. Only he could do these marvelous deeds, and his instrument was the most powerful force they knew. The notion of the wind as God's agent pervades the whole Old Testament. We read in Jeremiah these words of God: "I will scatter to every wind those who cut the corners of their hair . . ." (49:32);

---

[2] Friedrich Baumgärtel, in "Spirit of God," Bible Key Words (New York: Harper and Brothers, 1961), p. 3.

and in Isaiah: "But he [God] will rebuke them, and they will flee far away; chased like chaff on the mountains before the wind and whirling dust before the storm" (17:13). There is an intimate note in Psalm 135: " . . . he brings forth the wind from his storehouses" (v. 7), as if to make them part of God's domestic equipment. He travels "on the wings of the wind," and makes them his messengers (Ps 104:3-4). A primitive phenomenon well serves as a revelation of one of God's basic attributes. The Jews saw the *ruach* as simply the *ruach* of God.[3]

Another early manifestation of God's power, expressed by *ruach*, occurs noticeably in Judges: it is the spirit of God coming upon an individual to equip him for some specific act. We read in the account of Samson that a young lion attacked him, "And the Spirit of the Lord came mightily upon him, and he tore the lion asunder as one tears a kid" (Jgs 14:6). When the men of Judah were delivering Samson over to the Philistines, " . . . the Spirit of the Lord came mightily upon him, and the ropes which were on his arms became as flax that has caught fire, and his bonds melted off his hands" (Jgs 15:14). Prior to Samson, God had commissioned the young Gideon to deliver the Israelites from the tyranny of Midian. "The Spirit of the Lord took possession of Gideon . . ." (Jgs 6:34), and he led his people to victory. It was the power of God's *ruach*, for Gideon had protested concerning himself and his own qualifications: "Pray, Lord, how can I save Israel? Behold, my clan is the weakest in Manasseh, and I am the least in my family" (Jgs 6:15). The same thing happened to Jephthah: "The Spirit of the Lord came upon Jephthah . . . Jephthah crossed over to the Ammonites to fight against them, and the Lord gave them into his hands . . ." (Jgs 11:29, 32). Eichrodt writes thus in reference to these passages:

"It was precisely in the unexpected success of their enterprises that the Israelite recognized the activity of a higher power;

[3] Cf. 2 S 22:16; 1 K 18:12; 2 K 2:16; Ho 13:15; Is 4:4; 30:28; Ex 15:8; Is 40:7; 59:19; Jb 4:9; 26:13.

and by designating this power as ruach he made his political leaders the direct servants of the national God and the instruments by which the latter exercised his sovereignty."[4]

By now it is possible to see the ruach of God as an intermediary for power, a force used by God to achieve his ends. By means of the ruach as wind God manipulates his creatures; by the ruach as a special force which he gives to certain Israelite leaders, they are able to perform superhuman deeds which he has willed. It is in this sense that Christ designated the Holy Spirit as the Paraclete, which means in the Greek, a helper, or an intercessor, definitely a powerful intermediary between Father and Son and the Christian.

When Samuel anointed David as king to succeed Saul, " . . . the Spirit of the Lord came upon David from that day forward" (1 S 16:13). Again the ruach is given to a national leader so that he might carry out God's plan for Israel, the same as it was given to Gideon, Jephthah and Samson, but here we note a big difference: with these men the ruach was transient; with David it is permanent, abiding. God had intended his ruach to be permanent in Saul also, but when David was anointed king after God's rejection of Saul, " . . . the Spirit of the Lord departed from Saul, and an evil spirit from the Lord tormented him" (1 S 16:14).[5] I shall return to the notion of the abiding ruach because it is most important in the New Testament theology of the spirit. Here the matter is simpler: to see God's ruach as his power in men for action.

In all of these instances God gives his ruach to those whom he has chosen for a mission to his people, who are to rule them in some capacity. So we see the ruach given to the

---

[4] Walther Eichrodt, Theology of the Old Testament (Philadelphia: The Westminster Press, 1961), vol. I, p. 308.

[5] It is possible that these texts are post-exilic, and that the permanence of the ruach in David and Saul is a concept derived from passages such as Is 11:2, so that what was predicated of the Messiah-king was also predicated of his ancestor, and of all of David's successors. As to the latter passage, McKenzie has an enlightening note: " . . . the evil spirit is called the evil spirit of Elohim or the evil spirit from Yahweh, but not the evil spirit of Yahweh. . . ." John L. McKenzie, S.J., "Spirit," in Dictionary of the Bible (Milwaukee: The Bruce Publishing Company, 1965).

prophet Ezekiel, whose frequent mode of transportation was by the *ruach:* "The Spirit lifted me up and brought me to the east gate of the house of the Lord" (Ezk 11:1).[6] The Servant of Isaiah, who is none other than Christ, the head of his body which is the fulfillment of God's people, likewise, and most appropriately of all, receives the *ruach:* "The Spirit of the Lord God is upon me, because the Lord has anointed me . . ." (Is 61:1).[7]

It is understandable, then, that the prophets should receive God's word by means of his *ruach.* The first time that the *ruach* of God is connected with prophecy is in 1 S 10:5-6. Samuel has just anointed Saul king and gives him as a sign that he is truly God's choice for king, among other things, the fact that he will meet a group of prophets who will be prophesying to the accompaniment of musical instruments: "Then the spirit of the Lord will come mightily upon you, and you shall prophesy with them and be turned into another man." After Saul's rejection, when David was fleeing from him for his life, Saul heard that the king was with Samuel. "Then Saul sent messengers to take David; and when they saw the company of the prophets prophesying, and Samuel standing as head over them, the Spirit of God came upon the messengers of Saul, and they also prophesied" (1 S 19:20). The upshot of the matter is rather comical. After sending two more contingents to get David, who both ended up prophesying, Saul, "being exceedingly angry," decided to go himself. But the inevitable happened: " . . . the Spirit of God came upon him also, and as he went he prophesied, until he came to Naioth in Ramah" (19:23). The question that arises at this point is, what kind of prophecy is this anyway? Group-prophecy, and sung to orchestral accompaniment! The answer is quite simple: it was psalmody, the singing of God's praises. If these prophets had been Benedictines, we would say that they were singing the Divine Office. The Hebrew verb meaning to prophesy is *naba*, and in the above

---

[6] Cf. Ezk 3:14; 9:24; 37:1; 43:5.
[7] Cf. Lk 4:18-21; Is 11:1-5; 42:1.

passages it means to praise God in a ceremonious manner. The thing to note is that in order to do this as a prophet, or *nabi*, the *ruach* of God had first to come upon one. Again, it is the intermediary of God's power, enabling the prophet to carry out a God-oriented act.

The forerunners of the prophets were called seers, as was Samuel. The reason Saul met Samuel in the first place was to get information about his father's strayed asses.[8] Seers did not necessarily need the *ruach* to obtain their information, although when King Jehoram of Israel wanted to know from Elisha, who was a prophet, whether he and the king of Judah would defeat Moab, Elisha asked for a minstrel. "And when the minstrel played, the power of the Lord came upon him. And he said: Thus says the Lord . . ." (2 K 3:15). The power of the Lord here is tantamount to spirit of the Lord.[9] From what we know of the procedure of these early prophets, the psalmody, either of the minstrel or of Elisha, would prepare the latter for the coming of the spirit of God, or else be inspired by that spirit. Here is an instance of a prophet, not a seer, seeking to learn from God a future event, and he does so in the accepted prophetic mode, psalmody. The prophet, emerging as the mediator of God's word, takes over the earlier prophetic functions of seer and inspired singer, and he operates in all of them by means of the *ruach*. A century after Elijah and Elisha, Hosea can call a prophet "the man of the spirit [*ruach*]" (Ho 9:7). And a little later Micah writes: "the seers shall be disgraced, and the diviners put to shame; they shall all cover their lips, for there is no answer from God. But as for me, I am filled with power, with the Spirit of the Lord, and with justice and might, to declare to Jacob his trangression and to Israel his sin" (Mi 3:7–8). It is debatable whether the prophet as we know him, the man of God, such as Elijah, Isaiah, and Jeremiah, was a member of a group of prophets, such as those gathered about Samuel, and later attached to the Jerusalem

---

[8] Cf. 1 S 9:9, 11, 18.
[9] Cf. Ezk 3:14; 1 K 18:46.

temple.[10] If he was, his personal call by God gave him a new and national role, which became the predominant and characteristic one. Nevertheless, both forms of prophecy, group or ecstatic, and the individual prophecy of the delivered and written word, depend on the *ruach* of God.

The prophet is the man of the word of God, and his ability to receive that word is derived from the *ruach*. Hence, the constant association of the *ruach* with the prophet, or at least with the act of prophesying, in either of its forms. We read in Numbers that God gave Moses seventy elders to help him bear his burdens. " . . . [the Lord] took some of the spirit that was upon him [Moses], and put it upon the seventy elders; and when the spirit rested upon them, they prophesied" (Nm 11:25). Later Moses relates the *ruach* to prophecy: "Would that all the Lord's people were prophets, that the Lord would put his spirit upon them!" (Nm 11:29.) Balaam, a seer, who was not even an Israelite, was summoned by the king of Moab to curse the oncoming Israelites. "When Balaam saw that it pleased the Lord to bless Israel, he did not go, as at other times, to look for omens, but set his face toward the wilderness. And Balaam lifted up his eyes, and saw Israel encamping tribe by tribe. And the Spirit of God came upon him, and he took up his discourse and said . . ." (Nm 24:1–2), which turned out to be a blessing. An earlier prophet, Micaiah, foretold the death of Ahab, against Zedekiah, spokesman for the king's four hundred prophets, who had foretold victory. Immediately after " . . . Zedekiah the son of Chenaanah came near and struck Micaiah on the cheek, and said, 'How did the Spirit of the Lord go from me to speak to you?' " (1 K 22:24.) After the exile Zechariah, himself a prophet, could write of the source of the prophetic word: " . . . the law and the words which the Lord of hosts

---

[10] Cf. Walther Eichrodt, *op. cit.*, p. 339 f. Aubrey R. Johnson, *The Cultic Prophet in Ancient Israel* (Cardiff: The University of Wales Press, 1962), pp. 60–75; Curt Kuhl, *The Old Testament: Its Origins and Composition* (Richmond: John Knox Press, 1962), p. 157 f. Cf. the close relation of the psalms with prophetic preaching in Adam C. Welch, *The Psalter: In Life, Worship and History* (Oxford: Clarendon Press, 1926), pp. 89–118.

had sent by his Spirit through the former prophets" (Zc 7:12). In Sirach, one of the last of the Old Testament books, the connection of word and spirit is as clear as ever, only by this time the prophet had given way to the teacher of the Law and the temple singer: "If the great Lord is willing, he [the teacher of the Law] will be filled with the spirit of understanding; he will pour forth words of wisdom and give thanks to the Lord in prayer . . ." (BS 39:6).[11]

The reader has by this time missed passages from Isaiah, Jeremiah and Ezekiel, relating the *ruach* to their respective missions. The reason for their omission is that such passages do not exist. The early prophets were ecstatics: the *ruach* of God would come upon them, and they would praise God in song, and also dance. Sometimes the dancing would get pretty vehement, and the scene would somewhat resemble a session in one of our more emotional sects after the congregation has felt the coming of the "Spirit." We read that Saul, in an incident already referred to, under the influence of the *ruach*, removed his clothes and "lay down naked all that day and night" (1 S 19:24). As Dom Maertens explains:

"The prophetic spirit of these earlier 'possessed' was too much like the human exaltation that accompanies enthusiasm, drunkenness, or anger, and its manifestations greatly resembled the unbridled agitation to which the false prophets of Baal lent themselves."[12]

When we realize that there were numerous other prophets in ancient Israel, such as Ahab's four hundred, whose ecstatic behavior could have led to disedifying excesses, and that this behavior would, of course, be attributed to the *ruach* of God, it is not difficult to see why prophets like Isaiah and Jeremiah felt it better not to mention that the *ruach* came upon them. It could be that the Hebrews associated the conduct of pagan prophets, such as those of Baal, if not with the *ruach* of God, at least with some *ruach*, as a source of prophetic power.

---

11 Cf. 2 S 23:2; 2 Ch 15:1; 20:14; 24:20; Ne 9:30.
12 Thierry Maertens, O.S.B., *The Breath and Spirit of God* (Notre Dame: Fides Publishers, Inc., 1964), p. 38.

The frenzy of the latter mentioned in 1 Kings 18:28 would hardly create a "favorable image" of the *ruach* in the popular mind: "And they cried aloud, and cut themselves *after their custom* with swords and lances, until the blood gushed out upon them."[13]

Yet the very omission of the prophetic *ruach* in these two prophets is a clear affirmation of the association of the prophet with the *ruach*. During the exile, when the number of prophets had either diminished or been considered to be cultic officials, Ezekiel felt able to declare the source of God's word to him: "And when he spoke to me, the Spirit entered upon me and set me upon my feet; and I heard him speaking to me . . ." (Ezk 2:2–3); "Then the Spirit of the Lord fell upon me, and he told me to say: Thus says the Lord . . ." (Ezk 11:5). The behavior of Ezekiel during the time that he is receiving so many prophetic "words" is very definitely ecstatic, and although this may be due to his peculiar disposition, one wonders if ecstasy, produced by the *ruach*, is not the usual condition of the prophet in which to receive God's word. In his ecstasy he may speak certain words which make no apparent sense, *glossolalia*. Father Bourke is most enlightening on this matter: "Out of the prophet's incoherent *glossolalia* a 'word' wells up in his consciousness which seems to him of overwhelming significance. It emerges in the form of a brief enigmatic sentence, a phrase, or even a single word. The children's names in Osee and Isaias are obvious examples: *Lo-ruhawah* (You have not been granted mercy), *Maher-shalal-hash-baz* (Spoil-hastens-plunder-speeds), etc. Oracles grow up as explanations of the significance of these names. Or else the 'pregnant word' which subsequently forms the kernel of the oracle may take the form of a pun." He refers here to Amos 8:2, where the Hebrew for ripe fruit is quite like that for end, finish. Isaiah, too, employed the pun, namely in 5:7, and 7:9. "A marked preference can be discerned in these 'embryonic' oracles or 'pregnant words' for sibilant or

---

[13] For another reason for the omission of the prophetic *ruach* in Isaiah and Jeremiah, cf. Joseph Bourke, O.P., "The Spirit of God in the Old Testament," *The Life of the Spirit*, vol. 13, no. 156 (June, 1959), pp. 544 f.

guttural sounds. They are in fact usually the sort of words that one might have expected to burst from the lips of a frenzied man."[14] The names "Bonds" and "Favor" which Deutero-Zechariah gave his two shepherd staffs have all the ring of ecstatic words.

I have devoted much attention here to the prophets, but this has been necessary in order to fully understand the Old Testament meaning of God's *ruach*. A prophet is a mediator of God's word; he receives it from God and gives it to men. While the usual prophetic word is an oracle, a threat, a foretelling of success or doom, a blessing, it may also be one of praise of God, and while this at the time it is uttered is meant for God, may not many of them have been meant also for hearers, who remember them, and give them back to God in psalms? The intermediary power between God and the prophet, which puts the latter into an ecstasy, enabling him to receive the word, is the *ruach* of God. This *ruach* is always separable from the prophet; it is not his but God's. He cannot control it; on the contrary, the *ruach* controls the prophet, often with forceful activity. Without the *ruach* he is not a prophet.

THE SPIRIT OF GOD AS CREATIVE

"Then the Lord God formed man of dust from the ground, and breathed into his nostrils the breath of life, and man became a living being" (Gn 2:7). We have met this text before, in Chapter 4, where we were interested in the *nephesh hayyah*. Now we are interested in what causes man to be a living *nephesh*, and we see that it is God's breath. As I remarked above, breath here is not *ruach*, but the rarely used *neshamah*. However, the concept is the same — that breath and life are synonymous, and that man's life is the result of God's life and of his gratuitous gift of it. Later references to this drop *neshamah* in favor of *ruach*, such as: " . . . all flesh in which there is the breath of life" (Gn 6:17). If God is to give life outside of himself, it must be by his breath as the metaphor for his own eternal vitality and for its mode

---

[14] *Ibid.*, pp. 543 f.

of transmission. Thus God's ruach as breath is creative.[15]

The book of Job definitely expresses the relation between God's breath and the creation of man: "The spirit [ruach] of God has made me, and the breath [neshamah] of the Almighty gives me life" (33:4); "If he should take back his spirit [ruach] to himself, and gather to himself his breath [neshamah], all flesh would perish together, and man would return to dust" (34:14–15). The parallel use of neshamah in these passages serves to strengthen the concept of God's breath as being creative. Not only man, but all creation depends on this breath for existence: "By the word of the Lord the heavens were made, and all their host by the breath of his mouth" (Ps 33:6). By host here is meant the furnishings of space, the heavenly bodies. "O Lord how manifold are your works! . . . the earth is full of thy creatures. When thou hidest thy face, they are dismayed; when thou takest away their breath, they die and return to their dust. When thou sendest forth thy Spirit, they are created, and thou renewest the face of the earth" (Ps 109:24, 29–30). Breath and spirit here translate ruach; hence, we see that the life breath of creatures — and the psalm earlier mentions birds, badgers, lions and fish — is the life-giving breath of God.

Psalm 104 assigns not only creation, but also re-creation to God's breath, in the sense of renewal of life, replenishment and re-stocking with new creatures. If every year there are newborn animals, it is because of God's dynamic breath. We find a similar use of ruach in Psalm 51; only here the re-creation is moral: "Create in me a clean heart, O God, and put a new and right spirit within me. Cast me not away from thy presence, and take not thy holy Spirit from me. Restore to me the joy of thy salvation, and uphold me with a willing spirit" (vv. 10–12). The "new and right ruach" and the "willing ruach" are man's; they are his dispositions toward God. Yet they really are not his, but God's: "your holy ruach." As in Psalm 104, ruach is both God's and man's,

---

[15] Cf. William A. Barry, S.J., "Spirit as the Source of Life in the Old Testament," The Bible Today, no. 17 (March, 1965), p. 1104.

something of the creator in the creature to bring about and sustain life, only in Psalm 51 that life is one oriented to God. The *ruach*, as a substantial bond, directs a man's being and conduct in accord with God's will.

We know from the psalm that its author had not followed the leading of this *ruach*, that he had grievously sinned. He asks to be created anew as a man of God; hence he asks for a renewal of this God-orientating *ruach*. This thinking is a good step farther from that which considers the *ruach* to be the cause of mere physical life. Commenting on the passage cited, Friedrich Baumgärtel writes: "The Spirit of God is a creative, transforming power, and its purpose is to create a sphere of religion and morals."[16] After Saul was anointed king he had to experience a re-creation, and this, as Samuel told him, would be the work of the *ruach*: "And the Spirit of the Lord will come upon you, and you will prophesy with them, and will be turned into another man" (1 S 10:6).

Ezekiel has used more vividly than the others this concept of the re-vivifying *ruach* in his famous vision of the dry bones. " ' Thus says the Lord God to these bones: Behold, I will cause breath [*ruach*] to enter you, and you shall live. . . . and you shall know that I am the Lord. . . . Come from the four winds, O breath, and breathe upon these slain, that they may live.' So I prophesied as he commanded me, and the breath came into them, and they lived, and stood upon their feet . . ." (Ezk 37:5, 6, 9–10).

In the passage already quoted, Psalm 33:6, we notice, because of the typical parallelism, a relation between the *ruach* and the word of the Lord. Both are equally his creative agents. And in Psalm 143 the *ruach* and the word produce the same effects: "He sends forth his word and melts them [the frozen waters]; he makes the wind [*ruach*] blow, and the waters flow" (v. 18). The reason for this is that not only do both proceed from God's mouth, but the word is produced by his breath.

---

16 Friedrich Baumgärtel, *op. cit.*, p. 1.

GOD IS SPIRIT

We have seen *ruach* in the Old Testament as God's dynamic presence in creation, or, to put it more concretely, as his intermediary for power, whether it is the wind, or his breath taking hold of a man, empowering him for divinely guided action, or his breath enabling the prophet to hear the word of God. But this *ruach* in action also reveals what God is. We read in Isaiah: "The Egyptians are men, not God, their horses are flesh, not spirit . . ." (31:3). Canon Dewar thus comments on this passage: "Here men and flesh, and God and spirit are clearly parallel. In other words, flesh is the essence of man and spirit is (so to say) the essence of God."[17]

But what does the *ruach* have to tell us of God's being? First, it reveals that God is act, a dynamic, rather than static, being. Christ will reveal what that act is — Father and Son and the Breath of their love — but for the Old Testament it was sufficient to indicate the essential aliveness of God, that "our Lord is above all gods," who "have ears, but they hear not, nor is there any breath [*ruach*] in their mouths" (Ps 135:5, 17). Second, *ruach* reveals the power of God, that this dynamic God can do everything. In Isaiah we read: " . . . for the mouth of the Lord has commanded, and his Spirit has gathered them" (34:16. Note the parallel of the word and the spirit). And in Zechariah: "Not by might, nor by power, but by my Spirit, says the Lord of hosts" (4:6). The *ruach* hovering over the emptiness reveals the power of God, about to create (Gn 1:2). Third, it reveals him as love, and love that is not an abstraction nor a mere attribute, but again as something dynamic, as love loving. I would give here as another definition of God's *ruach*, his outgoing life. Finally, the Old Testament concept of God's *ruach* carries the notes of transcendence and immanence: a wind, a breath, that is above and superior to the people of God, belonging very particularly to God as his agent, and

---

[17] Lindsay Dewar, *The Holy Spirit and Modern Thought* (New York: Harper and Brothers, 1960), p. 5.

yet abiding with them as agent of his presence.[18] When
Christ said, "God is spirit" (Jn 4:24), this is what he meant,
God as essentially infinite dynamic power of love. And this
word of Christ in the New Testament perfectly sums up the
meaning of the *ruach* of God in the Old.

THE ABIDING SPIRIT

We have noticed throughout this chapter that the *ruach*
of God operates directly, or indirectly, for the national good.
That is to say, it operates to enable individuals to do their
part in carrying out God's plan for Israel, and through their
efforts, to inform the people what is God's will for them
here and now toward the fulfillment of his plan. If we ask
what that plan is, we must begin with Abraham, to whom
God promised a numerous offspring. This offspring, the
Israelites, God would bind to himself by the covenant. Paul,
by the fullness of revelation, tells us who Abraham's offspring really is: "It does not say, 'And to offsprings,' referring to many, but, referring to one, 'And to your offspring,'
which is Christ" (Gal 3:16). The people of God, bound by
the covenant, and bound more closely still by the kingdom,
looked forward after the fall of the kingdom to the apocalyptic
fact, the kingdom of the Messiah, which is the whole Christ.
This is the end of God's plan, and this is the end toward
which the *ruach* of God is working in the Old Testament.
It may seize young Samson so that he might save his life,
but its ultimate purpose is the formation of the body of
Christ. The Bible is Christ, as he himself tells us, and we
can only understand the *ruach* of God as ultimately the *ruach*
of Christ.[19]

The *ruach*, therefore, is power for human conduct that is
God-oriented. It would seize the whole man and direct him
to God — "spiritual" conduct. We shall study this later, but
here, in relation to it, we must study the Old Testament's
texts which speak of the *ruach* as abiding, permanent.

---

[18] Cf. Is 40:13–14.
[19] Cf. Lk 24:25–27, 32.

Let us first look at those texts which refer to specific individuals or groups. When God tells Moses to choose seventy elders to help him, he adds: "I will take some of the spirit which is upon you and put it upon them; and they shall share the burden of the people with you" (Nm 11:17). Here the bestowal of the *ruach* is once and for all, not a transient visitation. The same is true of the *ruach* given to the skilled vestment-makers: "And you shall speak to all who have ability, whom I have endowed with an able mind, that they may make Aaron's garments, to consecrate him for my priesthood" (Ex 28:3).[20] Joshua " . . . was filled with the spirit of wisdom, since Moses had laid his hands upon him" (Dt 34:9).[21] And later, in the time of the judge Othniel: "The Spirit of the Lord came upon him, and he judged Israel" (Jgs 3:10). Samuel anoints David king, "And the Spirit of the Lord came upon David from that day forward" (1 S 16:13). Attesting to the permanence of the *ruach* not only in David, but also in his anointed successors, are these words of Proverbs: "Inspired decisions are on the lips of a king; his mouth does not sin in judgment" (Pr 16:10).

What of the permanence of the *ruach* in the prophets? Elisha asks Elijah, before the latter's ascent: "I pray you, let me inherit a double share of your spirit" (2 K 2:9). Later, the sons of the prophet attest: "The spirit of Elijah rests upon Elisha" (2 K 2:15). We must remember that a prophet has been called by God to the prophetic state — the basic meaning of *nabi*, prophet, is *called*. The calls of Elisha (1 K 19:16), Isaiah (Is 6:1–13), Jeremiah (Je 1:4–9), and Ezekiel (Ezk 2), readily come to mind. One who is a prophet by state, or vocation, has the spirit "poured out" upon him, a type of the Spirit of Pentecost, to serve as a new principle of action. The giving a word to the prophet is, then, only one manifestation of the spirit's action upon him. To sum up: The *ruach* of God comes upon the prophet and remains with him,

---

[20] Cf. Ex 31:3–6.
[21] Cf. Nm 27:16–18.

but is operative for the purposes of the prophetic mission only on occasion.[22]

The activity of the *ruach* indicated to the Israelites the presence of God among them. Its phenomena were in themselves signs of his dynamic, and vitally interested, presence. They did not consider the *ruach* to be God, but his agent, and more, his activity on their behalf. Thus the presence of the *ruach* meant that God was among them, his people: " . . . take courage, all you people of the land, says the Lord; work, for I am with you, says the Lord of hosts, according to the promise that I made you when you came out of Egypt. My Spirit abides among you; fear not" (Hg 2:4–5). " . . . this is my covenant with them, says the Lord: my spirit which is upon you, and my words which I have put in your mouth, shall not depart out of your mouth, or out of the mouth of your children, or out of the mouth of your children's children, says the Lord, from this time forth and for evermore" (Is 59:21). "Cast me not away from thy presence, and take not thy holy Spirit from me" (Ps 51:11).[23]

"In a very special sense," writes William Barclay, "because Israel is the people of God, *Israel is the people amidst whom the Spirit of God dwells.* If the Spirit of God has a home upon earth, that home is admidst the fellowship of the people of God."[24] It is precisely because Israel is God's chosen people that he sends his *ruach* among them, that by means of it he is present to them. Therefore we see the *ruach* as the revelation of God's love for Israel. In all of its activities, whether those of power or the word, the Jews recognized God's love as the motive behind his interest in them. In Psalm 139 the psalmist is stunned with wonder at God's intimate knowledge of him, and he cries out: "Whither shall I go from thy Spirit? or whither shall I flee from thy presence? . . . Even there thy hand shall lead me, and thy right hand hold

---

[22] Cf. Dn 5:11, 12, 14. Although this portion of Daniel is in Aramaic, spirit translates Aramaic *ruach*.

[23] Cf. Ne 9:20; Is 63:14.

[24] William Barclay, *The Promise of the Spirit* (Philadelphia: The Westminster Press, 1960), p. 19.

me" (vv. 7, 10). It is, he knows, a loving knowledge, like that of a solicitous mother, and its evidence in his life is God's ruach. A passage from Third Isaiah beautifully relates God's ruach to his love of Israel: "I will recount the steadfast love of the Lord, the praises of the Lord, according to all that the Lord has granted us, and the great goodness to the house of Israel which he has granted them according to his mercy, according to the abundance of his love. . . . In his love and in his pity he redeemed them, he lifted them and carried them all the days of old. But they rebelled, and grieved his holy Spirit . . ." (63:1, 9–10). Whether in the personal or the national life, the ruach reveals God's love.

The Messiah — prophet, king, and priest — will be a man of the ruach, according to Isaiah: "The Spirit of the Lord shall rest upon him . . ." (11:2); "Here is my servant whom I uphold, my chosen one in whom my soul delights; I have put my Spirit upon him . . ." (42:1). Christ applied this passage to himself in the beginning of his ministry: "The spirit of the Lord God is upon me, because the Lord has anointed me . . ." (Lk 4:18–21. Cf. Is 61:1). The Messiah will be on the side of the poor and afflicted (11:4); he will "heal the brokenhearted," "comfort all who mourn" (Is 62:1, 2). In other words, the ruach of God in him will lead him to works of love and compassion. He will "bring glad tidings to the lowly" (62:1); the word of God he will receive, as a prophet, from the ruach of God.

But, more especially, he will receive the ruach because he will be the firstborn of the new people of God, the body of Christ. Heretofore, the unity of God's people was their national solidarity. The ruach was with them as God's presence. Now, in Messianic times, the basis for unity is organic union with Christ, with his body. Therefore presence of the ruach among the new people of God is the presence of the ruach in Christ as head. The Holy Spirit must first be in him, and because he is, he is with the Church. We see fulfilled these words of Isaiah, " . . . chosen in whom my soul delights; I have put my Spirit upon him . . ." (42:1) in these of Luke:

" . . . and the Holy Spirit descended upon him in bodily form as a dove, and a voice came from heaven, 'Thou art my beloved Son, in thee I am well pleased'" (3:22. Confraternity version). On Pentecost, among Peter's first words in his sermon immediately after the coming of the Holy Spirit were these prophetic words of Joel: "'Then afterward I will pour out my spirit upon all mankind. Your sons and daughters shall prophesy, your old men shall dream dreams, your young men shall see visions; even upon the servants and the handmaids, in those days, I will pour out my spirit' (cf. Jl 2:28–29). These men are not drunk, as you suppose, for it is only the third hour of the day. But this is what was spoken through the prophet Joel . . ." (Acts 2:15–16. Conf. tr.).

We have seen the meaning of the *ruach* of God in the majority of its contexts, and can conclude that it represents his power, his loving presence, his outgoing life, on behalf of his people. Like God's word, it reveals him. The meaning of the *Hagion Pneuma*, the Holy Spirit, can only be grasped in these Old Testament contexts. But they are just as absolutely necessary in order to understand the *ruach* of man, and, therefore, man.

CHAPTER 5

The Spirit of Man
in the Old Testament

In general the *ruach* of man means life, but exilic and post-exilic texts, in particular, recognize that this life comes from God and is directed to him. In view, then, of the fuller revelation, we can say that man's *ruach* is, chiefly, life from God.

In an early Genesis text we read these words spoken by God: "My spirit [*ruach*] shall not abide in man for ever, for he is flesh" (6:3). They refer, of course, to Genesis 2:7: "Then the Lord God formed man of dust from the ground, and breathed into his nostrils the breath of life, and man became a living being."[1] As Berkouwer says, "We may indeed call Genesis 2:7 the *locus classicus* of Old Testament anthropology, but not in the sense of showing a substantial dichotomy; but rather, as a revelation of man's complete createdness and dependence in his whole existence."[2] Man's life is, after all, God's *ruach*, his breath, which constituted him a human being in the first place, and preserves him in being, a breath that continues to be shared in what must be a mouth-to-mouth relationship. This is what is meant by life from God. We see this vividly illustrated by the hopelessly dead and scattered bones of Ezekiel's vision, to which the prophet speaks the word of the Lord: "I will lay sinews upon you, and cause flesh to come upon you, and cover you with skin, and put breath [*ruach*] in you, and you shall live;

---

[1] We would expect the word for breath here to be *ruach*, but it is *neshamah*, which word we shall consider later in the chapter. All subsequent references to this passage, however, have *ruach* instead.

[2] G. C. Berkouwer, *Man: The Image of God* (Grand Rapids: Wm. B. Eerdmans Publishing Company, 1962), p. 215.

and you shall know that I am the Lord" (Ezk 37:6). The *bashar* is not the source of human life, but the *ruach*, God's own breath.

God created man in his image (Gn 1:26-27). In the light of the *ruach* of God as meaning his outgoing life, cannot this image be the *ruach* which creates man, and which keeps him continually directed toward God? New Testament revelation will show that this is the best explanation of man as the image of God.

SPIRIT AS LIFE

In some of the oldest of the Old Testament texts in which *ruach* is applied to man, the meaning is simply vitality.[3] The queen of Sheba was so impressed with Solomon and his palace that " . . . she had no longer any spirit in her" (1 K 10:5). In two J (Yahwist) texts of pre-Amos date the meaning is also that of vitality, or power: "And God split open the hollow place that is at Lehi, and there came water from it; and when he [Samson] drank, his spirit [*ruach*] returned, and he revived" (Jgs 15:19); "And when he [an Egyptian] had eaten, his spirit [*ruach*] revived" (1 S 30:12). An E text, also pre-Amos, conveys the same concept: "And when he [Jacob] saw the wagons and all that he had sent, his spirit [*ruach*] revived" (Gn 45:27). This early meaning is not that of the later breath-soul, the vital principle, but only of vitality, akin to what we would call "pep." The relation between breath and life is readily grasped, but in these passages *ruach* is not the source of life but rather life itself.

Because a man is alive he breathes. *Ruach* can also mean simple animal respiration, as in this early text: "Everything on the dry land in whose nostrils was the breath of life died" (Gn 7:22). This text harks back to Genesis 6:3, but does not indicate the source of the breath. Moreover, from

---

[3] I have found invaluable the detailed monograph of Daniel Lys, *Ruach: Le Souffle dans L'Ancien Testament* (Paris: Presses Universitaires de France, 1962). Dr. Lys has classified every *ruach* passage according to time of composition, and analyzed each meaning.

the context we see that all animals have this *ruach*, "from reptile to bird of the air" (7:23). Habakkuk says derisively of an idol: "Behold, it is overlaid with gold and silver, and there is no breath [*ruach*] at all in it" (Hab 2:19). And Coheleth observes: "There is no man who is master of the breath of life so as to retain it, and none has mastery of the day of death" (Ec 8:8).[4] But the Hebrews could see their respiration theocentrically; it was, after all, God's gift: " . . . and the dust returns to the earth as it once was, and the life-breath returns to God who gave it" (Ec 12:7).

Since *neshamah* means breath of life in Genesis 2:7 and elsewhere, what is the relation between it and *ruach*? The "narrow physical sense" of breath is conveyed by *neshamah*, that is, breath and nothing more.[5] Too, it signifies calm, peaceful breathing, as against *ruach*, which means breath that comes through the nose, agitated and violent. The use of both words as synonyms, as in the case of *ruach* and *nephesh*, is not common before the exile.[6] But even as synonyms, the meaning of *ruach* wins out, as in these passages: "As long as my breath [*neshamah*] is in me, and the spirit [*ruach*] of God is in my nostrils . . ." (Jb 27:3); "If he [God] should take back his spirit [*ruach*] to himself, and gather to himself his breath [*neshamah*], all flesh would perish together, and man would return to dust" (Jb 34:14–15); "Thus says God, the Lord, . . . who gives breath [*neshamah*] to its people . . . and spirit [*ruach*] to those who walk in it" (Is 42:5). Man's vital breath is God's gift; he breathes "by courtesy" of God.

"The idea of power involved in the word *ruach* is carried over into what we would now call psychology, to denote the dominant impulse or disposition of an individual," writes

---

[4] Cf. Ezk 37:6; Is 42:5; Je 10:14; 51:17; Gn 6:17; Ec 3:19, 21; Ps 104:29.

[5] Cf. *The Interpreter's Dictionary of the Bible* (Nashville: Abingdon Press, 1962), vol. 1, p. 465. Also H. Wheeler Robinson, *The Christian Doctrine of Man* (Edinburgh: T. and T. Clark, 1947). According to Robinson, *neshamah* occurs only twenty-four times in the Hebrew Bible (pp. 15–16), as against *ruach's* 378 (pp. 17–18).

[6] Cf. Aubrey R. Johnson, *The Vitality of the Individual in the Thought of Ancient Israel* (Cardiff: University of Wales Press, 1949), p. 31.

Norman Snaith.[7] That, and the idea of life, I would add. A living person has at least one drive that dominates him, or at least tries to, and which he must dominate by means of another drive. This is often expressed in the Old Testament by *ruach*. Hosea complains that "the spirit of harlotry" has led the priests astray (Ho 4:12). Ezekiel prophesies woe to " . . . the foolish prophets who follow their own spirit, and have seen nothing" (Ezk 13:3). "Then all the congregation of the people of Israel departed from Moses. And they came, every one whose heart stirred him and every one whose spirit moved him, and brought the Lord's offering to be used for the tent of meeting, and for all its service, and for the holy garments" (Ex 35:21). "If the spirit of jealousy comes upon him, and he is jealous of his wife . . ." (Nm 5:14). Akin to this last is "the spirit of confusion" (Is 19:14). A right disposition toward God is the "willing spirit" of Psalm 51:14. And an important theme of Ezekiel, to which I shall return, is expressed in this verse: "Cast away from you all the transgressions which you have committed against me, and get yourselves a new heart and a new spirit!" (Ezk 18:31.)[8] From this sampling we can see that the range of drives is quite wide.

There is a group of texts that speak of God's "stirring up," or raising, the spirit of a man so that he will determine upon some course of action that God wills. "Sharpen the arrows! Take up the shields! The Lord has stirred up the spirit of the kings of the Medes, because his purpose concerning Babylon is to destroy it" (Je 51:11). "And the Lord stirred up the spirit of Zerubbabel, the son of Shealtiel, governor of Judah, and the spirit of Joshua the son of Jehozadak, the high priest, and the spirit of all the remnant of the people; and they came and worked on the house of the

---

[7] Norman H. Snaith, *The Distinctive Ideas of the Old Testament* (New York: Schocken Books, 1964), p. 146. Snaith points out the relation between *ruach* as a man's drive and the wind as a powerful force.

[8] Cf. Ho 5:4; Dt 2:30; Nm 14:24; 27:18; Is 29:24; Zc 13:2; Jb 32:18.

Lord of hosts, their God . . ." (Hg 1:14).[9] In these cases *ruach* is the determining or dominating drive.

Not as strong as this drive, but nonetheless influential in a man's conduct, are his dispositions, his habitual attitudes. Again, *ruach* represents these. "But this is the man to whom I will look, he that is humble and contrite in spirit, and trembles at my word" (Is 66:2). "A man's pride will bring him low, but he who is lowly in spirit will obtain honor" (Pr 29:23). "The patient in spirit is better than the proud in spirit" (Ec 7:8). "But when his heart was lifted up and his spirit was hardened . . ." (Dn 5:20).[10]

In many passages *ruach* stands for the seat of the emotions, which is logical, considering the relation of our drives, dispositions, and emotional states. In an early, pre-Amos text *ruach* means anger: "their anger [*ruach*] against him abated" (Jgs 8:3). A Proverbs text has the same meaning for *ruach*: "He who is slow to anger is better than the mighty, and he who rules his spirit [*ruach*], than he who takes a city" (16:32). So also one in Coheleth: "If the anger [*ruach*] of the ruler rises against you . . ." (Ec 10:4). The word can mean courage: "And as soon as we heard it, our hearts melted, and there was no courage [*ruach*] left in any man . . ." (Jos 2:11); " . . . there was no longer any spirit in them, because of the people of Israel" (Jos 5:1). In a number of uses the meaning is sadness: "The Lord calls you back, like a wife forsaken and grieved in spirit . . ." (Is 54:6). "The Lord is near to the brokenhearted, and saves the crushed in spirit" (Ps 34:18).[11]

By now it is apparent that a great similarity exists between the *ruach* and the *nephesh*; some may be tempted to see an identity. The similarity and difference between the two words I shall take up in the third section of this chapter, after we have studied the deeper meanings of *ruach*.

---

[9] Cf. Is 19:13; Pr 18:14; Ez 1:1, 5; 1 Ch 5:26; 2 Ch 21:16; Ps 78:8; 1 Mc 13:7.

[10] Cf. Is 57:15; Ec 7:9; Ps 51:12, 19; 76:13.

[11] Cf. Ezk 21:12; Ex 6:9; Is 61:3; 65:14; Dn 7:15; Ws 5:3.

THE RUACH AS POWER FROM GOD

God's ideal for Israel was the prophetic state. Joel prophesied of messianic times: " . . . I will pour out my spirit on all flesh; your sons and your daughters shall prophesy, your old men shall dream dreams, your young men shall see visions. Even upon the menservants and maidservants in those days, I will pour out my spirit" (2:28–29). Peter, in his first sermon on Pentecost day, declared that the Pentecostal coming of the Holy Spirit was the fulfillment of this prophecy, and thus indicated who this general prophetic Spirit would be. Everyone of the new people of God would operate by means of this special power of God and would be a prophet in the sense that "led by the Spirit of God" he would be able to live as a son of God (Rm 8:14). Each one would know the word of God, live by it, and declare it; or, rather, know the Word, live by him, and bear witness to him.

In the last chapter we saw that God gave his ruach to judges, such as Gideon and Jephthah, and to David and his successors, so that they could perform acts willed by him in accordance with their state. Today we would call this the "grace of state." The ruach of God inspired the prophets with God's word, and remained with them as a source of his power in their state of men of God and of the word. That this abiding ruach was not the same as the ruach in them which was their breath, the seat of their emotions, and their dominating drives is quite obvious. The former was God's, the latter, theirs. And yet, the latter was not theirs, as later revelation especially brings out. The concept of man's ruach comes to connote, along with the other meanings, life given by God that orients the person to him, that is, power for life according to God's will. This concept parallels that which makes God's ruach abide in men, rather than coming in transient visitations. Hence, Joel's prophetic ruach of God for all will find a receptive and willing ruach of man with which to operate.

The early Genesis text, 6:3, made it clear that man's ruach was in reality not his, but God's, as did Genesis 2:7: Commenting on this latter text, Father Dominique Barthélemy writes:

> "But this breath which causes him to exist does not belong to man. Human breath is the breath of God exhaled into the nostrils of statuettes which he has modelled from moistened dust. . . . In effect, only the breath of God animating man assures the provisional coherence of the dust to which man will return when this breath will have left his lips. . . ."[12]

Professor Snaith has the same comment, but adds a logical conclusion:

> "The ruach is given him by God; it is God's neshamah (breath). When this ruach returns to God, then man's dust returns to the earth. . . . The division is man and flesh on the one side, God and ruach on the other."[13]

A remark of G. C. Berkouwer is pertinent here:

> "The characteristic of the biblical view [of man] lies precisely in this, that man appears as related to God in all his creaturely relationships. The biblical portrayal of man, as a religious portrayal, also emphasizes that this relation to God is not something added to his humanness; his humanness depends on this relation."[14]

Since a man's breath is actually God's, it is associated with God. Although man needs ruach to be a human being, a living nephesh, it is really not he. Not in a hostile sense, but in that of division, a man's ruach is in opposition to man, who is bashar and nephesh, but strictly speaking is not ruach, in the sense that the latter is a purely natural component or viewpoint. But because he needs the ruach for his human existence, a man has thereby a natural, "built-in," orientation to God, that necessarily creates a relation to him, and, as Berkouwer almost wryly puts it, " . . . his humanness depends on this relation." So the ruach as the life-breath

---

[12] Dominique Barthélemy, O.P., "Le Souffle du Dieu Vivant," La Vie Spirituelle, Apr., 1963, p. 445.

[13] Norman H. Snaith, op. cit., p. 150.

[14] G. C. Berkouwer, op. cit., pp. 195–196.

works both ways: it keeps a man human, and it keeps him turned toward God, the source of his *ruach*.

Let us look at some later texts which treat of the *ruach* as life from God. Those most akin to Genesis 2:7 and 6:3 are in post-exilic books, particularly Job. "The spirit [*ruach*] of God has made me, and the breath [*neshamah*] of the Almighty gives me life" (Jb 33:4). Man's *ruach*, we know, is God's *neshamah*. "If he should take back his spirit [*ruach*] to himself, and gather to himself his breath [*neshamah*], all flesh would perish together, and man would return to dust" (Jb 34:14–15). There is also the passage from Coheleth, already quoted in this chapter: "And the dust returns to the earth as it was, and the spirit [*ruach*] returns to God who gave it" (Ec 12:7). God is called the "God of the spirits of all mankind," in Numbers 16:22; 27:16.[15] Dust is something to which a man is naturally akin, and he is dust in common with all animals. But while he is also *ruach*, it is, in the last analysis, only loaned to him, and as long as it enlivens him, he is akin to God.

Thus the life-breath that gives a man vitality, respiration, emotions, and drive, since it is God's, has more than just these natural functions: it is man's supernatural power. We read in Ezekiel these words of God concerning the exiled Israelites: "I will give them one heart and put a new spirit within them; I will take the stony heart out of their flesh and give them a heart of flesh, that they may walk in my statutes, and keep my ordinances and obey them; and they shall be my people and I will be their God" (11:19–20). The heart, we will recall from Chapter 4, is also a center of volition; the new spirit will insure its willing what God wills. This verse is related to 11:5 where, in the Hebrew, wicked thoughts are ascribed to the *ruach* of man: " . . . for I know the wicked thoughts of your *ruach*." As a result, the Israelites did not keep God's ordinances (11:12). With a new *ruach* they will. In Ezekiel 18:31 there is the same idea with a different "twist": "Cast away from you all the transgressions

---

15 Cf. Jb 10:12; 12:10; Mal 12:15; Zck 12:1.

which you have committed against me, and get yourselves a new heart and a new spirit." This new spirit is the result not only of God's action — his "grace" — but also of man's cooperation. God can give power but man must "cast away" and "get," if there is to be a renewal of his proper relationship with God.

It was known from the earliest time of Israel's history that a man's ruach, since it was not his, kept him dependent upon God, and created a relationship that can only be described as a life that was totally controlled by God. This is implied in the Genesis texts. But it was not until shortly before the exile that it was made explicit in the above-quoted texts of Ezekiel. These are the first statements that a man's ruach orients him to God in order that he might do God's will. They are the first specific indications that the ruach is power for such conduct. The fact that they were understood demonstrates the attitude of the Israelites toward the ruach. We can recognize here a similarity between it and the ruach of God given to national leaders and prophets.

But we recognize in these texts of Ezekiel a cognate meaning of ruach — that of a man's driving and determining power — a meaning that derives from ruach as life-breath and also wind. This is clear from its parallel position with the heart.

Later in Ezekiel we find a development. "A new heart I will give you and a new spirit I will place within you, and I will take out of your flesh the heart of stone and give you a heart of flesh. And I will put my spirit within you, and cause you to walk in my statutes and be careful to observe my ordinances. You shall dwell in the land which I gave your fathers; and you shall be my people, and I will be your God" (36:26–28).[16] This passage is identical with 11:19–20, with one noticeable exception: in the earlier passage the restored Israelites will observe God's ordinances by means of their own renewed ruach; in the later, they will do this by means of their renewed ruach as well as by God's ruach.

---

[16] Cf. Ezk 37:14; Ps 51:12, 13.

There is no idea here of a substitution — of God's ruach for man's, but of a cooperation. Before God gives his ruach, he must first give man a renewed, receptive ruach. Of course we can see here man's ruach as being in reality God's, but the meaning, in the light of similar texts, is that God's ruach in this passage is similar to the prophetic spirit. At about the same time God speaks to the exiled Israelites through Second Isaiah: "I will pour out my spirit upon your off-spring" (Is 44:3). The ruach of Joel 2:28 is the prophetic ruach. The development of the theology of the ruach of man which Ezekiel 36:27 contributes is not only that a man's ruach is naturally oriented to God, and, therefore, the whole man himself, but also that a man lives his God-ward orientation practically by means of God's ruach. There-fore he partakes of the ruach of judges, kings, and prophets. This is what is meant in Zechariah: "I will pour out on the house of David and on the inhabitants of Jerusalem a spirit of compassion and supplication . . ." (12:10). "For the spirit of the Lord now becomes the principle of godly conduct," writes Father Barry, "the principle of life in its more pro-found sense of conformity to God's own life."[17]

Several post-exilic texts see the God-oriented ruach as the seat of understanding and wisdom, thus being the perfect instrument of God's ruach. "But it is the spirit [ruach] in a man, the breath [neshamah] of the Almighty, that makes him understand" (Jb 32:8). Note here that man's breath is not considered to be his, but God's. "And my intelligent spirit replies to me" (Jb 20:3. The Complete Bible). "For wisdom, the fashioner of all things, taught me. For there is in her a spirit that is intelligent, holy . . . and interpenetrating all spirits that are intelligent, pure, and most subtle" (Wis 7:22, 23. The Complete Bible). This passage echoes the words of Wisdom in Proverbs: "Lo! I will pour out to you my spirit, I will acquaint you with my words" (1:23). So the ideal fundamental relationship between God and man is that

---

[17] William A. Barry, S.J., "Spirit as the Source of Life in the Old Testa-ment," The Bible Today, no. 17 (March, 1965), p. 1108.

of spirit to spirit, actually that of the prophet, man of God and of the spirit.[18]

The Spirit of God that dwelt in the prophet is to dwell in the ordinary individual, the layman, to serve as his directive force, as creative power, as a new principle of Godward life. Parallel with this Spirit is that which makes the individual capable of receiving and of cooperating with it, namely, his own spirit. Developing revelation conceives of the spirit of man as man oriented to God, as created for and fulfilled by union with God. The spirit of the above-quoted passage from Job, "But it is the spirit [ruach] in a man, the breath [neshamah] of the Almighty, that makes him understand," is a far cry from Samson's spirit which revived after he had had a drink of water (Jgs 15:19). With the exception of Genesis 6:3, and its related verse, 2:7, the concept of the spirit of man before Ezekiel is of something as personal and natural to him as his ears or eyes. It is power, drive, vitality, but as natural as the nephesh. With Ezekiel this driving force becomes God's breath, which, although natural and necessary to a man as man, is in reality God's, and as such gives him a supernatural power and orientation.

The notion of man's ruach as God's breath did not burst upon Israel in the time of Ezekiel as something new, no more than did the doctrine of the Mystical Body in the twentieth century. It was understood by the Hebrews before this time, but apparently not emphasized. With the deeper realization of this basic relationship between God and man by Ezekiel and others, contemporary and later, man's ruach was seen as that in man which made his life not only by, but also for, God.

Thus the spirit of man provides the medium for the activity of the prophetic, or charismatic, spirit. This latter, which abides with the prophet, will abide with everyone for Godward conduct. With the decline of prophecy, the vocation of all to the prophetic state, because of the abiding ruach of God, becomes a possibility in messianic times. Joel's spirit poured

---

[18] Cf. 1 K 17:24; 2 K 1:9–13; 4:9, 22, 25, 27; Ho 9:7.

out on all mankind (2:28–29) is realized at last on Pentecost, which opened the era of every-man-a-prophet.

DIFFERENCES AND SIMILARITIES

From our survey of the above texts, no one can say that the ruach of God is identical with that of man. Yet there is a similarity that must be examined. For example, in Ezekiel's vision of the dry bones ruach is used for the prophetic spirit that comes upon the prophet (37:1), the breath that brings the bones to life (37:5, 6, 8, 9, 10, 14), and the winds that are the source of the life-breath (37:9).[19] The similarity is really quite obvious: ruach is breath, and in these passages it is God's breath inspiring the prophet, the wind as God's breath, which then is seen as the logical source of the life-breath of man. Ruach, after all, is only a metaphor, and it is used here for three different things, although each is said to be breath. What does the metaphor express? Life, and basically God's life. In this, then, there is a similarity between God's ruach and man's. Ruach, whether it means God's, inspiring and sustaining the prophet and king, or the life-breath of man, represents God's breath in man in the sense of his vitality, life. Since God's life is God, God-centered, his ruach in man is the power centering man on God, enabling him to relate his life to God. The ruach of man is the same as the ruach of God only as the rays of the sun shining in a room are the same as the sun. Only in this sense is the ruach of man by its nature the same as that of God.

What is the relation between man's ruach and his nephesh? There would seem to be some confusion of the two terms in passages such as these: "My soul [nephesh] yearns for thee in the night; my spirit [ruach] within me earnestly seeks thee . . ." (Is 26:9); "I will speak in the anguish of my spirit [ruach]; I will complain in the bitterness of my soul [nephesh]" (Jb 7:11); " . . . because he failed to know the one who formed him and inspired him with an active

---

[19] Cf. Thierry Maertens, O.S.B., *The Breath and Spirit of God* (Notre Dame: Fides Publishers, Inc., 1964), pp. 54–55.

soul [*psychē*], and breathed into him a living spirit [*pneuma*]"
(Ws 15:11). The parallelism in these passages equates both
terms, it is true, but we must remember the way it is with
words. An original meaning develops other related meanings
in the course of years. Certain of these may predominate at
a certain time, or in a particular region. One meaning which
may represent quite a development of the original can have
relevance for the mentality of a period, as for example that
of "encounter" today, with its own context and consequences.
What happened to *ruach* is that it underwent such a development. From the original meaning of breath, or wind, it came
to denote God's creative power, the breath of God in man
which keeps him alive, strong emotion, the dominant force
in man, and, from the exile on, the life-principle of man.
Thus this later meaning coincides with the later meaning of
nephesh.[20]

But there is a difference. *Ruach*, despite appearances, does
not have quite the same meaning as *nephesh*, even in the
texts in which they occur as parallels. Wheeler Robinson
wrote: " . . . the higher associations of the *ruach* of God,
developing with the conception of God himself, serve, on the
whole, to keep the use of the term for human psychology
at a higher plane of meaning than that of *nephesh*."[21] This
higher plane of meaning depends on the difference between
the radical concepts which each word conveys: the *nephesh*,
after all, is man's vital principle, his breath-soul, that which
makes him a living being; the *ruach* is God's gift of this same
life, God's creative and sustaining breath which causes man
to be a breathing, living, being. The difference is clearly indicated in Genesis 2:7. As Edmond Jacob so well puts it:
"*Nephesh* is what results when *bashar* is animated by *ruach*."[22]
Nephesh represents merely natural man, which *ruach* generally does not. The very idea of the latter term is the activity

---

[20] Cf. *The Interpreter's Dictionary of the Bible*, vol. 4, pp. 428–429; 432.
Also H. Wheeler Robinson, *op. cit.*, pp. 17–20.

[21] *Ibid.*, p. 20.

[22] Edmond Jacob, *Theology of the Old Testament* (London: Hodder and
Stoughton, 1958), p. 161.

of God in man: "As you do not know how the spirit [ruach] comes to the bones in the womb of a woman with child, so you do not know the work of God who makes everything" (Ec 11:5).

We can say that the nephesh is the principle of life relative to the person, and that the ruach is the principle of life relative to God. Both terms designate human life and are hence co-extensive, but ruach adds a new dimension, the God-ward, for it indicates that this life is breathed by God and is directed to him.

Although the parallel use of ruach and nephesh, as well as the exchange of either word for the other, can certainly be attributed to the linguistic development of these words, I think that the basic reason for such "confusion" results from the deeper realization of man's ruach as being God's breath. Since emphasis was placed on the fact that a man's life is directly from God, in a "mouth-to-mouth" relationship, then life, or nephesh, can easily be called what it actually is, ruach. This latter term does indeed describe a person as forceful, driving, determining, it is true, but underlying its later use for man is its theocentric meaning.[23]

The contrast between ruach and bashar is by now quite apparent: it is that between God and man, the divine and the human, the supernatural and the natural. Two passages from Walther Eichrodt will highlight this contrast:

"It is significant that from the time of Isaiah onwards conduct that is truly in accordance with God's will is included in the category of ruach, that is to say, it is a manifest effect of the miraculous divine life, while all that is merely human belongs to the sphere of bashar, the transient and creaturely."

---

[23] As to the use of "spirits" for the souls of the dead in the places, especially pseudepigraphic, mentioned in Chapter 3, n. 29, we can conclude that as the nephesh is seen to be separable from the bashar, and as the ruach is more and more realized to be life from God, it is logical that this separable life be called "spirit." There is not question here of the immateriality of the disembodied soul, of its "spiritual" substance, nor of natural vitality or power. The basic meaning of "spirit" in these instances is simply God's breath, at least implicitly understood.

He thus comments on Isaiah 31:3:

" 'Spirit' is the inexhaustible power of the divine life, in which all life takes its origin; and bashar is the life of earth, which is essentially transitory and, like everything earthly and created, exhibits no new principle of life in itself. This contrast, however, appears in a new light, when the ruach is associated with the ethical factor. Yahweh's divine life, exalted over all created things, rests at its deepest level on moral perfection. The opposition between the permanent and the transitory world is in the last resort a conflict between the moral will which forms the world and that which is attached to egoistic and material ends."[24]

The bashar is a man's link with material creation; it is man as material creation, incapable as such of rising above it, earthbound and horizontal. The ruach is the same man, but capable because of it of reaching above the created to union with the Creator, able to elevate his milieu and himself, and be elevated, to a Godlike life. Bashar is incapable of choosing God, of a supernatural act. The ruach of man is something of God in man that chooses God, who necessarily has to choose himself. The great lesson of the Old Testament is that man, who is ruach as well as bashar, has to choose God. When he doesn't, he is doomed, not only as one of the people of God, but also as a human being. C. G. Jung wrote in a different context: "Religion, as the careful observation and taking account of certain invisible and uncontrollable factors, is an instinctive attitude peculiar to man, and its manifestations can be followed all through human history."[25] He may not have known it, but he was giving a good defense of the ruach of man.

By way of concluding this chapter, I would like to say that the Israelites did not see the ruach as the soul, as the nephesh was eventually considered to be. It was always life and power from God, even when the sacred writers spoke

---

[24] Walther Eichrodt, Theology of the Old Testament (Philadelphia: The Westminster Press, 1961), vol. I, pp. 388, 215–216.
[25] C. G. Jung, The Undiscovered Self (New York: The New American Library, 1961), p. 36.

of it in connection with emotions and understanding. A man's *nephesh* was an individual thing, or, rather, the individual was a *nephesh*. On the contrary, his *ruach* was not: there was only *one ruach*, not millions, as was the case with the *nephesh*, because there was only one breath of God. It may have been the principle that gave him life, but it was not the life-principle that he became because of God's breath.

CHAPTER 6

The Spirit of Man
in the New Testament:
Christ the Man of the Spirit

If the subtitle of this chapter strikes the reader as a bit puzzling, we have to remember that in the New Testament, as contrasted with the Old, we are in for some "jolts." The New Testament alone gives us the fullness of revelation, and the basic truth which Christ revealed was that about God. In the Old Testament, the emphasis was on God as *personal;* now Christ reveals that God is three persons: the Father, the Son, and the Holy Spirit. He is the eternal Son, become man at a definite point of time. And the Spirit — the Mediator-Intercessor — is a divine Person. This is not to say that the Old Testament Spirit of God was really the personal Holy Spirit in every case, yet with regard to the Spirit of prophetic inspiration it was, as New Testament passages which we shall consider affirm.

Christ also revealed the truth about man. Paul neatly summed this up when he referred to Adam as " . . . the type of him who was to come" (Rm 5:14). Christ is the real head of the human race, not Adam, who was only a type, a foreshadowing. Heretofore we have considered Adamic man, or man as Adam. From Christ on we must consider man as Christ. This is the fullness of revelation about man, his nature, meaning and end. This is the only true anthropology. Just as the Old Testament anthropology was incomplete, but true as far as it went, so the contributions of the various modern physical and social sciences are incomplete, although true as far as they go, as to what man really is. Man

really is *Christ*, and we shall study this New Testament revelation in this and the next two chapters.

In the New Testament the deeper significance of man's
ruach is made clear; its true ultimate purpose is disclosed.
The Spirit who abides in Christ abides in the man who is
"in Christ" — the Pauline phrase — and his *ruach* is his point
of contact with the Spirit: "It is the Spirit himself bearing
witness with our spirit that we are children of God" (Rm
8:16). The immediate effect of the redemption is the giving
of the Spirit, who " . . . dwells with you, and will be in you"
(Jn 14:17). Christ first gives the Spirit who is in him, and
then, through him, all the good things he has merited.[1] If the
highest meaning of man's *ruach* in the Old Testament is his
basic orientation to God, this is only a type again, a type of
that capacity for union with the Holy Spirit so great and
so real as to result in the union called, by Paul, the body of
Christ.

But the fact of the Spirit abiding in Christ and in his new
human race seems to have a precedent in the prophets upon
whom the *ruach* of God descended and remained. After all,
the prophet is the man of the Spirit par excellence in the Old
Testament, and the abiding Spirit is most closely associated
with him. That is precisely the New Testament point: Christ
is *the* prophet of the people of God; the men of the Spirit
of the Old Testament were, like Adam, only types. He comes
to pour out the Spirit that is in him, the "more abundant
life" of John 10:10.

Part of this complete revelation about man is that which
states the absolute necessity of re-creation. Every man is
conceived and born as Adamic man, but this is not enough.
He must be born again, of water and the Spirit, in order to be,
not man again, but Christ. And as creation was the work
of the *ruach* of God hovering over the emptiness, and of the
same *ruach* causing dust to be a living *nephesh*, so this re-
creation is the work of the personal Spirit, who acts through
the natural agent of the water.

---

[1] Cf. Lk 11:13; Mt 7:11.

While it may seem that this chapter should have been titled "The Spirit in the New Testament," I repeat what I wrote above: actually man is now Christ, or is meant to be, and can only be viewed from this standpoint. The relation of the ruach to man has to be its relation to Christ, and we know from our texts that the ruach of God is a person. We know know that the relationship which must exist is that already stated by Ezekiel in the composite of texts, 11:19–20, 18:31, and 36:26–28, studied in the last chapter: a close Spirit-to-spirit rapport; and which Joel foresaw as ideally existing when he said: "I will pour out my Spirit [ruach] upon all flesh" (2:28; cf. Acts 2:17–21).

Christ as Prophet

All of the evangelists wish it to be clearly understood that the Spirit has come upon Christ. "And when he came up out of the water, immediately he saw the heavens opened and the Spirit descending upon him like a dove" (Mk 1:10).[2] All four recount this descent after Christ's baptism. Luke also refers to it in Acts: "[You know] how God anointed Jesus of Nazareth with the Holy Spirit and with power. . . " (10:38). Both Matthew and Luke attribute the conception of Christ to the Spirit: " . . . she was found to be with child of the Holy Spirit;" "That which is conceived in her is of the Holy Spirit" (Mt 1:18, 20); "The Holy Spirit will come upon you, and the power of the Most High will overshadow you" (Lk 1:35).

Luke especially stresses the fact that Christ is a prophet, and that, therefore, Christians are prophets. At the beginning of Acts he gives the prophetic source of the word of God in Christ: "In my former book, Theophilus, I spoke of all that Jesus did and taught from the beginning until the day on which he was taken up, after giving instructions through the Holy Spirit to the Apostles whom he had chosen" (1:1–2). Later he refers to "the Spirit of Jesus" (16:7). Peter regards the prophets of the Old Testament as types of Christ the

---

[2] Cf. Mt 3:16; Lk 3:21; Jn 1:33.

prophet when he states that these spoke only out of the
Spirit of Christ: "The prophets who prophesied of the grace
that was to be yours searched and inquired about this salvation; they inquired what person or time was indicated by
the Spirit of Christ within them when predicting the sufferings of Christ and the subsequent glory" (1 Pt 1:10–
11).

Thus Christ is impelled, directed, by the Spirit. "And
Jesus, full of the Holy Spirit, returned from the Jordan, and
was led by the Spirit for forty days in the wilderness, tempted
by the devil" (Lk 4:1–2).[3] "And Jesus returned in the power
of the Spirit into Galilee . . ." (Lk 4:14). With the Holy
Spirit as his power " . . . he went about doing good and
healing all that were oppressed by the devil, for God was with
him" (Acts 10:38). Matthew sees Christ as Isaiah's Servant
of Yahweh, who acts by means of the Spirit: "I will put my
Spirit upon him, and he shall proclaim justice to the Gentiles" (Mt 12:18; Is 42:1). More important still is Christ's
application to himself of Isaiah's words: "The Spirit of the
Lord is upon me, because he has anointed me to preach good
news to the poor. . . . Today this scripture has been fulfilled
in your hearing" (Lk 4:18, 21).

Christ himself said that he was a prophet: "A prophet is
not without honor, except in his own country, and among
his own kin, and in his own house" (Mk 6:4). He was
so considered by the people: "It is a prophet, like one of
the prophets of old" (Mk 6:15). " 'Who do men say that
I am?' And they told him, 'John the Baptist; and others say,
Elijah; and others one of the prophets' " (Mk 8:28). And on
Palm Sunday, at the end of his ministry: "And when he entered Jerusalem, all the city was stirred, saying 'Who is this?'
And the crowds said, 'This is the prophet Jesus from Nazareth of Galilee!' " (Mt 21:10–11.)

Yet it can be objected that Christ cannot be a prophet because the latter receives the Spirit from God, whereas the
Spirit was always in him as God the Son. This is the very

---

[3] Cf. Mt 4:1; Mk 1:12.

reason why Christ is *the* prophet, all his predecessors having been types. He is the man of the Spirit in the truest sense of the word because of his essential union with the Holy Spirit. As man he received the Spirit at the instant of his conception; or rather, the human nature joined to the person of the Son was so joined by the Holy Spirit. And the same Spirit comes upon him at the Jordan, investing him with his prophetic mission. Note the insistence of all four evangelists on this "anointing" by the Spirit, which to them paralleled the calls and investitures of Elisha, Isaiah, and Jeremiah. The human nature of Christ is henceforth dependent on the Holy Spirit during the years of his ministry, just as were the old prophets. The big point in the evangelists' unanimity in recounting the descent of the Spirit on Christ is that just as the prophets lived by the Spirit, so does Christ. But, unlike the prophets, Christ is for those of his body the source of the Spirit. John beautifully unites these two facts: "He on whom you see the Spirit descend and remain, this is he who baptizes with the Holy Spirit" (Jn 1:33). The other three evangelists give the statement of John the Baptist that Christ will baptize with the Holy Spirit, but only John relates this giving of the Spirit with Christ's own prophetic "anointing." Thus John sees baptism as the call of the Christian to the charismatic state of the prophet.[4]

Christianity restores the prophetic tradition. Dr. Filson writes: "In the work of John the Baptist and Jesus, the priestly element is again subordinated to the prophetic accent. The same attitude characterizes the apostolic writings generally."[5] As to John the Baptist, he is clearly a prophet, even as to his wearing the traditional outer garment of the prophets, the melōtes: "A prophet? Yes, I tell you, and more than a prophet"

---

[4] Cf. Mt 3:11; Mk 1:8; Lk 3:16. Actually confirmation, as the completion of the work of baptism, confers this "anointing," baptism being the union of the person with the Incarnation of Christ. As such baptism is truly the call to the prophetic vocation, although remotely, having the same relation as Christ's incarnation had to the visible coming of the Spirit upon him. Cf. my *Led by the Spirit* (Milwaukee: The Bruce Publishing Company, 1965), pp. 86–109.

[5] Floyd V. Filson, *The New Testament against its Environment* (London: SCM Press, Ltd., 1959), p. 85.

(Lk 7:26–27).[6] His prophetic call is related by Luke in language that is reminiscent of the call of Jeremiah: "He will be filled with the Holy Spirit even from his mother's womb" (Lk 1:15).[7] After a lapse of some three centuries a prophet again arises, to be the precursor of a charismatic religion.

The Christian as Prophet

Several texts state that the Holy Spirit was the *ruach* that inspired the utterances of the charismatic leaders of the Old Testament. The word of Christ affirms this: "David himself, inspired by the Holy Spirit, said . . ." (Mk 12:36). And Peter declared: "Brethren, the scripture had to be fulfilled, which the Holy Spirit spoke beforehand by the mouth of David, concerning Judas . . ." (Acts 1:16). And in the second epistle of Peter we read concerning the prophets: "no prophecy ever came by the impulse of man, but men moved by the Holy Spirit spoke from God" (2 Pt 1:21).[8]

A larger number of texts says the same thing with regard to Christians. First, Luke reports of the Pentecostal outpouring of the spirit of God: "And they were all filled with the Holy Spirit and began to speak in other tongues, as the Spirit gave them utterance" (Acts 2:4). This recalls the *ruach* coming upon Saul and the prophets in 1 Samuel 10:10, whose prophecy was the praise of God. But more particularly the event is the fulfillment of Joel's prophecy, as Peter, immediately afterward, attests, quoting the passage: "But this is what was spoken by the prophet Joel: 'And in the last days it shall be, God declares, that I will pour out my Spirit upon all flesh, and your sons and your daughters shall prophesy, and your young men shall see visions, and your old men shall dream dreams; yea, and on my menservants and my maidservants in those days I will pour out my Spirit; and they shall prophesy'" (Acts 2:16–18[Jl 2:28–29]).[9] The gospel, the new word

---

[6] Cf. Mt 3:4; Mk 1:6; 2 K 1:8.

[7] Cf. Je 1:5.

[8] Cf. Acts 4:25; 7:51; 28:25.

[9] Notice that where Joel has "in these days" in verse 29, Peter substitutes "in the last days," knowing with the authority of the newly given Spirit that Joel was referring to Messianic times. Cf. also Is 32:15; 44:3; 59:21; Ezk 36:25–27; 39:29. I shall return to these texts later.

of God, is then preached " . . . through the heaven-sent Holy Spirit" (1 Pt 1:12), who is the source of the word.

Through baptism the prophetic Spirit abides in the Christian. At the end of his first sermon on Pentecost, Peter's listeners asked: " 'Brethren, what shall we do?' And Peter said to them, 'Repent, and be baptized every one of you in the name of Jesus Christ for the forgiveness of your sins; and you shall receive the gift of the Holy Spirit' " (Acts 2:37–38). The Christian is said to be "full of the Holy Spirit" (cf. Acts 6:5; 7:55; 13:52), and this is his usual condition: "Did you," Paul asks some Christian disciples at Ephesus, "receive the Holy Spirit when you believed?" When they confess their ignorance of the Spirit's existence, and Paul learns that they had received only John's baptism, " . . . they were baptized in the name of the Lord Jesus. And when Paul had laid his hands upon them, the Holy Spirit came on them; and they spoke in tongues and prophesied" (Acts 19:2–6). God's indication to Peter that the Gentiles also should receive baptism was the coming of the Holy Spirit upon Cornelius and his household before they were baptized (cf. Acts 10:44–47; 11:4–18; 15:8).

Because the Christian is filled with the Spirit, it is the Spirit who does the speaking when it is a matter of witnessing to Christ. Jesus tells this to the Apostles: "For it is not you who speak, but the Spirit of your Father speaking through you" (Mt 10:20).[10] An example of this is seen in the case of Stephen and his disputants: "But they could not withstand the wisdom and the Spirit by which he spoke" (Acts 6:10). The Church increases in numbers "in the comfort of the Holy Spirit" (Acts 9:31).

This same Spirit of prophecy guides the early Church, indicating the divine will. It is the Spirit who tells the deacon Philip to attach himself to the Ethiopian official (Acts 8:29); and Peter allows himself to be taken to Cornelius' house at the instruction of the Spirit, as he admits (Acts 10:19; 11:12). The Spirit warns of a coming famine (Acts 11:28), tells Paul not to go to Jerusalem through the Christians at Tyre (Acts

---

[10] Cf. Mk 13:11; Lk 12:11–12.

21:4), and indicates Paul and Barnabas for a missionary jour-
ney (Acts 13:2).[11] As John resoundingly sums it up: "Let him
who has ears listen to what the Spirit says to the assemblies"
(Rev 2:7, etc.).[12] As Filson notes,

> "The fact of the Spirit's presence and aid is so frequently noted
> in the New Testament that it obviously is a common point in
> the experience and teaching of the Apostolic Church. We have
> no evidence of a section of the Church which did not know
> the gift of the Spirit. . . . Moreover, just as in the case of the
> relation to the risen Christ, the relation to the Holy Spirit
> included all of life."[13]

In view of the above-quoted texts, and others cited in the
notes, we conclude that the evangelists, Luke in particular,
regard the gift of the Holy Spirit as charismatic, as source
and power for the Christian in his relations with the Father,
with Christ, and with creation. The Spirit is to the Christian
what he was to the prophets. As I said above, Christ has restored the *prophetic* tradition.

This restoration is one of the basic reasons for his clash with
the Pharisees and the Scribes. From the time of Ezra (c. 445–
390 B.C.) the Law was supreme to the Jews. Without a king,
and with prophecy on the wane and the temple services
formalized, this is understandable. Professor Anderson writes:
"Ezra, then, gave great impetus to the development of 'legalism' — the strict conformity to Law — which came to be one
of the major characteristics of post-exilic Judaism."[14] The
Scribes or lawyers, as commentators and teachers of the Law,
assumed the importance and status formerly accorded to the
prophets. The Pharisees, the group of the "strict observance,"
were, along with the professional lawyers, devoted not only to
the Law, but also to the many oral traditions that had arisen
in connection with it, interpretations which adapted it to

---

11 Cf. Acts 15:28; 20:23; 21:11.
12 Cf. Acts 13:4; 16:6–7; 10:28.
13 Floyd V. Filson, *op. cit.*, p. 72.
14 Bernhard W. Anderson, *Understanding the Old Testament* (Englewood
Cliffs. N. J.: Prentice-Hall, Inc., 1957), p. 457.

later times.[15] We are familiar with Christ's upbraiding the Scribes and Pharisees over the Corban: " . . . and thus you render null and void the word of God by your traditions — a tradition which you are handing down. And you do many other things similar to these" (Mk 7:13; Kleist tr.).

"In Rabbinic thought," writes Erik Sjöberg, " 'the Spirit' is essentially the prophetic Spirit which speaks in the Old Testament. All the writings in the Old Testament are inspired by the Spirit. . . . Consequently, a saying from the Old Testament can be quoted either as a saying of the Torah or as a saying of the Holy Spirit."[16] This is, of course, true, but one can easily see what happened when prophecy as such declined. The authority of the charismatic Spirit was transferred to the Law. In fact, the charismatic Spirit is subordinated to the Spirit inspiring the Law. We sense this subordination in the following saying of one of the rabbis: "Moses received the Law from Sinai and committed it to Joshua, and Joshua to the elders, and the elders to the Prophets; and the Prophets committed it to the men of the Great Synagogue [the Sanhedrin]."[17]

The following statement by R. H. Charles, the great student and editor of apocalyptic literature, may be too extreme, but it at least indicates this trend away from prophecy:

"This absolute supremacy of the law [as seen in the books of Ezra, Nehemiah, and Deutero-Zechariah] carried with it . . . the suppression of prophecy — at all events of the open exercise of the prophetic gifts. And yet these gifts persisted during all the so-called centuries of silence — from Malachi down to New Testament times, but owing to the fatal incubus of the law these gifts could not find expression save in pseudepigraphic literature."[18]

---

[15] Cf. Floyd V. Filson, op. cit., pp. 83 f., William Foxwell Albright, From the Stone Age to Christianity (Garden City: Doubleday and Company, Inc., 1957), pp. 354–357; C. K. Barrett, The New Testament Background (New York: Harper and Row, Publishers, 1961). pp. 139–153.

[16] Erik Sjöberg, "Spirit of God," in Bible Key Words (New York: Harper and Brothers, Publishers, 1961), vol. III, pp. 7–8.

[17] C. K. Barrett, op. cit., p. 139.

[18] R. H. Charles, The Apocrypha and Pseudepigrapha of the Old Testament (Oxford: Clarendon Press, 1913), vol. II, p. 1.

Professor Anderson would not entirely agree:

"Finally, we must not suppose that there was a sharp antithesis between the Law and the prophetic tradition. . . . Far from repudiating the ethical demands of the prophets, the priests of Judaism attempted to 'put teeth' into prophetic teaching."[19]

But their method of doing so was insistence on the Law, as H. H. Rowley, quoted by Anderson, says:

"It is very doubtful if Ezra thought of this religion [Judaism] as in any way the antithesis of prophetic religion. He doubtless thought he was serving the ideals of the prophets, and embodying them in the Law, that they might achieve more than the preaching of the prophets had hitherto achieved."[20]

What was at stake was not so much the matter or content of the Hebrew faith, but the manner of the presentation. In any event, there was at length an antithesis between the Law and the prophets, and this antithesis sprang from a basic fact: a life led by the Spirit has to be spontaneous and free. As Professor Filson writes:

" . . . this life is of such a nature that it necessarily excludes the rule of an authoritative code of law. While Christians sometimes understand the legal regime of Judaism in too rigid a way, it remains true that the revealed will of God, embodied in his law and in the legal framework of life, exercised a commanding control which the rule of the Spirit does not permit."[21]

In this sense prophecy became subordinated to the Law, prophecy stood over against the Law and vice versa. In this regard it is interesting to note the Chronicler's alliance of prophets with the cult, and with the musical part of it in particular. For example: "And Chonenias chief of the Levites presided over the prophecy, to give out the tunes: for he was very skillful" (1 Chr 15:22; Conf. tr. cf. 15:27; 25:1–8).

What is Christ's attitude toward the Law? Father Wikenhauser has perfectly summarized this:

---

[19] Bernhard W. Anderson, op. cit., pp. 459–460.
[20] H. H. Rowley, The Rediscovery of the Old Testament (Philadelphia: The Westminster Press, 1946), p. 166.
[21] Floyd V. Filson, op. cit., p. 82.

"Jesus has come not to destroy but to fulfil the Law and the Prophets (Mt 5:17), that is, to perfect it by setting forth love, even love of one's enemies, as the totality of the divine will (Gal 5:14; Rm 13:8–10). Because of this thought, which is peculiar to him, Matthew begins his account of the work of Jesus with the Sermon on the Mount where Jesus appears as the new Lawgiver, the new Moses who proclaims the Old Testament law, in this new interpretation, as binding on the new people of God. It has been pointed out that Jesus does this from a mountain, just as Moses once climbed Sinai."[22]

When he declared that the fulfillment of the Law is love, Jesus did away with the individual prescriptions, and thereby put his interpretation of the Law above that of the professional Scribes. Furthermore the love of which he speaks is charismatic: " . . . God's love has been poured into our hearts through the Holy Spirit which has been given to us" (Rm 5:5). Christ's quarrel with the Law arises not from the Law itself but from what Judaism has made of it. Rabbinical tradition said, in effect, keep the Law and as a reward God will give you the Spirit. Jesus says, receive the Spirit and as a result you will be able to do God's will.[23] It comes down to the charismatic, or prophetic, Spirit vs. a legalism that is an end in itself.[24] The Law has served its purpose with the coming of Christ, who henceforth is the new Law through the Spirit.

This rather lengthy treatment of Christ and the Law has been necessary in order to understand the Spirit whom he came to give — the Spirit of the prophets, whom the adherents of the Law recognized as their enemy. We must return to the subject of the Christian as prophet, able now to realize better the new man whom Christ was creating.

We have studied the concept of the Holy Spirit in a selection of texts relative to Christ and the Christian as prophet, mainly from the synoptic writers; with this background we

---

[22] Alfred Wikenhauser, New Testament Introduction (New York: Herder and Herder, 1960), p. 189.

[23] Cf. Erik Sjöberg, op. cit., pp. 8–10.

[24] Ethelbert Stauffer treats of Christ's breaking of the sabbath laws in his pamphlet, Jesus and the Wilderness Community at Qumran (Philadelphia: Fortress Press, 1964), pp. 28–34.

can turn now to consider the spirit of man. The New Testament, as did the Old Testament, recognizes this spirit as man's orientation to God. This is seen particularly in the epistles of Paul which we shall take up in the next chapter. Christ tells the Apostles in Gethsemane: "The spirit [pneuma] indeed is willing, but the flesh [sarx] *is weak*" (Mt 26:41). John the Baptist " . . . grew and became strong in spirit [pneuma] . . ." (Lk 1:80). Luke tells us in Acts that Apollos " . . . was an eloquent man, well versed in the scriptures. He had been instructed in the way of the Lord, and being fervent in spirit [pneuma], he spoke and taught accurately the things concerning Jesus, though he knew only the baptism of John" (18:24–25). Although Peter uses pneuma in the sense of the separable soul in his first epistle, 3:19, in the previous verse the word means the supernatural principle: " . . . Christ . . . that he might bring us to God, being put to death in the flesh [sarx] but made alive in the spirit [pneuma]" (3: 18). In this verse pneuma cannot mean the soul, because Christ's resurrection — "made alive in the spirit" — was the reunion of his body and soul. Pneuma here is best expressed by Paul, writing of the risen Christ: " . . . but the life he lives he lives to God" (Rm 6:10). Peter has expressed this later, without mentioning the word, as living "according to the will of God" (1 Pt 4:2). He contrasts sarx, as the human condition with its exigencies, with pneuma, but with a beautiful new shade of meaning: " . . . but may live as God lives in spirit" (1 Pt 4:6, Conf. tr.). As God's life is necessarily knowing and loving himself, so the life of the spirit is knowing and loving God. Peter's use of the adjective, pneumatikos, has the same meaning: "And like living stones be yourselves built into a spiritual house, to be a holy priesthood, to offer spiritual sacrifices acceptable to God through Jesus Christ" (1 Pt 2:5). This "spiritual house," if we take the next two verses into consideration, is nothing else but the body of Christ. This is not something immaterial, or "spiritual" in the popular sense, but the human and the created lifted off the plane of the horizontal to be Christ.

SIMILARITIES AND DIFFERENCES

Other Old Testament meanings of ruach-pneuma also occur in the New. It represents the dominant disposition, " . . . the inner life of the heart, in the imperishableness of a quiet and gentle spirit, which is of great price in the sight of God" (1 Pt 3:4. Conf. tr.). Or desire: "Blessed are the poor in spirit . . ." (Mt 5:3). It is the seat of the other emotions: "And he sighed deeply in his spirit . . ." (Mk 8:12); Paul's "spirit was provoked" at the idolatry in Athens (Acts 17:16); Christ "groaned in his spirit," when he saw Lazarus' sister and friends weeping at his death (Jn 11:33); and he was "troubled in the spirit" over the betrayal by Judas (Jn 13:21). Pneuma is also the seat of knowledge: "And immediately, Jesus perceiving in his spirit that they thus questioned within themselves . . ." (Mk 2:8). Finally, it can mean the vital principle: "But after the three and a half days, a breath of life from God entered them [two dead witnesses]" (Rev 11:11).

This is the meaning of Christ's giving up his spirit at his death (Mt 27:50; Lk 23:46). The spirit here is not the soul, but simply the breath of life.[25] We have met this concept before in Job: "If he were to take back his spirit to himself, withdraw to himself his breath, all flesh would perish together, and man would return to dust" (34:14–15); also in Ecclesiastes: " . . . and the dust returns to earth as it once was, and the life-breath returns to God who gave it" (12:7).

Luke and Mark state that Christ gave up his breath, exepneusen, which is correctly translated by "expired," when that word is both literally and biblically understood. Stephen's dying request that Christ receive his pneuma must be understood in this sense (Acts 7:59). Christ's restoration of life to Jairus' daughter is marked by the return of her pneuma, her life-breath (Lk 8:55). And when James writes: "For just as the body without the spirit is dead . . ." (2:26), he

---

[25] In Lk 23:46 Christ quotes Psalm 31:6. The meaning in the psalm is that the person commits his life and welfare to God to whom he belongs. Christ's use of this passage shows the Old Testament realization that the breath of life belongs to God. See the texts quoted, Jb 34:14–15; Ec 12:7.

means the life-breath; there is no foundation, in spite of the juxtaposition of "body," for taking "spirit" as the soul.

The well-known parallelism of soul and spirit in Mary's Magnificat — "My soul magnifies the Lord, and my spirit rejoices in God my Savior" (Lk 1:46–47) — has its counterpart, as we have seen, in the Old Testament (Is 26:9; Jb 7:11; Ws 15:11). The reason for this parallelism is the similarity of concepts contained in both psychē and pneuma.[26] But we see something else in Peter's use of "spirits" in this passage: "In the spirit . . . [Christ] went and preached to the spirits in prison" (1 Pt 3:19). Is Peter using pneuma to express the separable soul? In view of his use of pneuma to mean man's supernatural tendency in 1 Peter 4:6, quoted above, I think not. What seems more probable is that he is merely using popular terminology, derived from apocalyptic literature. However, something more has to be said about this.

In the apocryphal Book of Jubilees (which Professor Albright dates in the early third century B.C.[27]), we read: "And their [the righteous'] bones shall rest in the earth, and their spirits shall have much joy. . . ."[28] And in I Enoch: "I saw the spirits of the children of men who were dead, and their voice went forth to heaven and made suit." "This is the spirit which went forth from Abel, whom his brother Cain slew, and he makes his suit against him till his seed is destroyed from the face of the earth. . . ."[29] II Enoch, a work of the first century A.D., however, sees the soul in the traditional Old Testament conception: " . . . his soul [comes] from my breath and from the wind."[30] A recent work on

---

[26] However we find in the Dead Sea Scrolls spirit meaning the soul, e.g., " . . . perfect in spirit and body and prepared for the day of vengeance," in J. Van Der Ploeg, O.P., Le Rouleau de la Guerre (Leiden: E. J. Brill, 1959), p. 42; "Unto God Most High are all the works of righteousness and way of a mortal is not established save through the spirit [which] God fashioneth for him" (Hymns, 4:31, in Menahem Mansoor, The Thanksgiving Hymns [Leiden: E. J. Brill, 1961]), pp. 151–152.

[27] Cf. W. F. Albright, op. cit., p. 347.

[28] Book of Jubilees, 23:31, in R. H. Charles, op. cit., vol. II, p. 49.

[29] I Enoch, 22:5, 7, in R. H. Charles, op. cit., vol. II, p. 202. "Spirit" also occurs in this sense in verses 9, 11, 12 and 13. Cf. also I Enoch 22:3–4; 98:3, 10.

[30] II Enoch, 30:8, in R. H. Charles, op. cit., vol. II, p. 449.

apocalyptic literature has these valuable observations: " . . . the terms 'soul' and 'spirit' have been drawn more closely together in the apocalyptic writings. The difference between them is not primarily one of kind but rather of aspect or approach, the spirit being expressive of that side of man's nature which may be more readily influenced by the spirit of God. We may say that 'soul' and 'spirit' together express the inner life of man in its lower and higher aspects respectively. . . . Both 'soul' and 'spirit,' then, are used to describe a normal element in human consciousness and yet they are distinct, not only in their origin, but in the fact that 'spirit' describes human nature in its higher affinities and in its Godward aspect."[31]

Because of the apocalyptic writings, then, Peter's readers knew what he meant, i.e., separable souls. Calling them "spirits" was common enough and, strictly speaking, meant nothing. It was a matter of popular terminology, not of any change in the meaning of *pneuma*.

To bring this chapter back to its leading idea — that in the New Testament the *pneuma* of man meets the *pneuma* of God, who is God, in an abiding charismatic relationship — the words of C. H. Dodd are most apt:

> "It is apparently the idea of prophetic inspiration that lies behind the doctrine of Jewish eschatology that the Messiah, or the People of God in the age to come, or both, will be invested with the divine *pneuma*; and this doctrine provided the mould for primitive Christian ideas. The tradition of the early Church, largely embodied in the apostolic *kerygma*, and attested in the Synoptic Gospels and the Acts, declares that John the Baptist had predicted a baptism *en pneumati hagio*, that Jesus was 'anointed' *pneumati hagio*, that during this ministry He promised *pneuma hagion* to his disciples, and that after His resurrection this promise was fulfilled."[32]

---

[31] D. S. Russell, *The Method and Message of Jewish Apocalyptic* (Philadelphia: The Westminster Press, 1964), pp. 155, 149.

[32] C. H. Dodd, *The Interpretation of the Fourth Gospel* (Cambridge: University Press, 1963), p. 222. I have transliterated the Greek words.

CHAPTER 7

The Spirit of Man
in the New Testament:
Spirit to Spirit

Of all the biblical writers Paul has contributed most to the understanding of man's spirit. *Pneuma* is " . . . the most important word in St. Paul's psychological vocabulary, perhaps in his vocabulary as a whole."[1] He has employed it 146 times, vastly more than any other author.[2] Yet he was not writing a professed anthropology or psychology; what Paul has written about man's spirit is in the service of his basic doctrine of man's union with Christ. This union, physical and total — the body of Christ — is supernatural to man. It supposes as a necessary *fundamentum* a man who is supernaturally oriented, created for and capable of this union. It needs a common ground on which union is possible, a something of God in man that can find fulfillment in the union of man with God. This meeting-place and radical orientation is the spirit. Paul stresses the role of the Holy Spirit in uniting the person to Christ: his role in the Christian life is that which he has, or rather, is in the life of God, the Trinity — union. Hence, according to Paul the Christian life results from a Spirit-to-spirit relationship.

FLESH AND SPIRIT

The Pauline use of *spirit* first strikes us in antithesis to *flesh*. We are most familiar with this passage from Galatians:

---

[1] H. Wheeler Robinson, *The Christian Doctrine of Man* (Edinburgh: T. and T. Clark, 1947), p. 109.

[2] *Ibid.*

"For the flesh lusts against the spirit, and the spirit against the flesh; for these are opposed to each other, so that you do not do what you would" (5:17, Conf. tr.).

Henry Barclay Swete's comment on this and related passages, although written years ago, is still valid:

> "But what is the spirit in antithesis to the flesh thus understood? Apparently not the Holy Spirit regarded as a Divine Person, nor simply the activity of the Spirit in men, but the higher side of human nature when by the power of the Divine Spirit it is set free from the domination of the flesh . . . the spirit then as well as the flesh in St. Paul's antinomy are both human, but the human spirit lies dormant and powerless till it has been awakened and enabled by the Spirit of God."[3]

The distinction is between Spirit-directed and ego-directed man. This is evident from the "works of the flesh" and the "fruit of the Spirit" in verses 19–23.

Another extended juxtaposition of flesh and spirit occurs in Romans 8:3–13. "For those who live according to the flesh set their minds on the things of the flesh, but those who live according to the Spirit set their minds on the things of the Spirit. To set the mind on the flesh is death, but to set the mind on the Spirit is life and peace" (vv. 5–6). The relation between flesh and death, spirit and life, occurs also in Galatians: "For he who sows to his own flesh will from the flesh reap corruption; but he who sows to the Spirit will from the Spirit reap eternal life" (6:8). This is reminiscent of Luke 9:24: "For whoever would save his life will lose it; and whoever loses his life for my sake will save it." Life here translates psychē, which like sarx, means living on the natural level; in other words, life that is ego-directed. Hence, to live an ego-directed, self-centered, life is to frustrate oneself as a human being, to deny oneself fulfillment as a person. Death in the literal sense, yes, plus all those things for which the word death is a graphic metaphor, summed also by "corruption." To sow in the spirit is to

---

[3] Henry Barclay Swete, The Holy Spirit in the New Testament (London: Macmillan and Co., Ltd., 1910), p. 395.

live according to God, God-directed and centered. This results in supernatural, as well as natural fulfillment — life, and the integrity and harmony which Paul calls "peace." Note that the passage from Galatians has "he who sows to his own flesh." This brings out the fact that living according to the flesh is living one's own life, without reference to God. *Own* is missing in connection with Spirit; the text reads simply, "he who sows to the Spirit." "This is only another way of saying that the standard of the Spirit, according to which a man directs his life, is not a potentiality of his own, but is given to him from outside himself."[4] Instead of a dichotomy, a tension, which results in the triumph of one and the annihilation of the other, spirit controls, supernaturalizes, a man's natural life. When Paul says that by the Spirit we must put to death the deeds of the flesh (Rm 8:13), he does not mean that the natural needs of human nature are to be denied it, but that man must not live in isolation from God. He is against living according to the flesh, which ignores and in practice denies God.

It can certainly be argued that in these passages (Rm 8:3–13 and Gal 5:17–23) *pneuma* is not the human spirit but the Spirit of God, and so the Revised Standard Version understands the term. In this case, then, Paul is opposing flesh to the Spirit. However, there is actually no fundamental opposition between spirit and Spirit, when we consider the flesh as representing man in his weakness and condition as creature, and the spirit as the divine in man — his breath that is his and yet God's. We need only recall the classic passage of Isaiah: "The Egyptians are men, not God, their horses are flesh, not spirit" (31:3). Flesh is equated with men, spirit with God. Or Ezekiel: "A new heart I will give you, and a new spirit I will put within you. . . . I will put my spirit within you and cause you to walk in my statutes and be careful to observe my ordinances" (36:26–27). Thus the "spiritual" life is a cooperation of God's Spirit and man's,

---

[4] Eduard Schweizer, "Spirit of God," in *Bible Key Words* (New York: Harper and Brothers, Publishers, 1961), vol. III, p. 76.

or rather, man's spirit is fulfilled and made operative only by God's Spirit. The former exists only for and by the latter.

"What comes from God is 'spirit,'" writes Father Grossouw:

> "what characterizes the man who arbitrarily wishes to remain by himself and to dispose autonomously of his own self and of the domain of visible nature is the flesh. That is the meaning of 'living to the flesh,' regardless of whether this desire for following one's own will in disobedience to the Creator expresses itself as licentiousness or as an idealistic moral-spiritual existence."[5]

The last part of this sentence would condemn "character training" and "personality development," even "striving for perfection," which are carried out on the purely natural level of self-improvement, without reference to God. All good, yes, but not good enough, since the flesh is to be directed by the spirit, at all times and in all things.

Charles Davis clearly states the biblical meaning of flesh and spirit:

> "He [Paul] is thoroughly Hebrew in outlook; he saw man simply as a unity. Consequently his antithesis of flesh (sarx) and spirit (pneuma) is not an opposition between matter and spirit, between body and soul. 'Flesh' is not part of man; but the whole man in his weakness and mortality, in his distance from God, and in his solidarity with a sinful and corrupt creation. 'Spirit' is man as open to the divine life and as belonging to the sphere of the divine, man under the influence and activity of the Spirit. Flesh and spirit are two active principles affecting man and struggling within him."[6]

"Walk by the Spirit, and do not gratify the desires of the flesh" (Gal 5:16).[7]

THE GODWARD DIMENSION

From Paul's opposition of flesh and spirit we know that

---

[5] W. K. Grossouw, *Spirituality of the New Testament* (St. Louis: B. Herder Book Co., 1961), p. 126.

[6] Charles Davis, "The Resurrection of the Body," *Theology Digest*, 1960, p. 100.

[7] Cf. 2 Co 7:1; 1 Co 9:11; 3:1.

one of the meanings which man's spirit has for him is a dimension, an orientation toward God, a faculty that is the principle of supernatural conduct. As Claude Tresmontant well puts it:

> "The spirit is man's participation in the supernatural order. . . . Hence the spirit-flesh opposition does not work a duality within nature itself as does the dichotomy of body and soul. It is in fact a distinction between the order of nature and the supernatural which is a revealed order."[8]

This is the same meaning which we discovered in the Old Testament texts which developed Genesis 2:7 and 6:3, texts such as Ezekiel 11:19; spirit is God's breath in man — God's and yet man's — serving as a *lien* between the two, turning man Godward, not earthward. And though this breath is natural to man, it supernaturalizes him in the sense of making him a capacity for God, to be filled only by God.

The *pneuma* enables a person to serve God: "For God is my witness, whom I serve with my spirit in the gospel of his Son . . ." (Rm 1:9). But the expression "serve with my spirit" seems to indicate a faculty, akin to the intellect and will, that enables a man to serve God as he deserves. We sense this idea of a supernatural faculty in the following passages: "For one who speaks in a tongue speaks not to men but to God; for no one understands him, but he utters mysteries in the Spirit. . . . For if I pray in a tongue, my spirit prays but my mind is unfruitful. What am I to do? I will pray with the spirit and I will pray with the mind also; I will sing with the spirit and I will sing with the mind also. Otherwise if you bless with the spirit, how can any one in the position of an outsider say the 'Amen' to your thanksgiving when he does not know what you are saying?" (1 Co 14:2, 14-16). Praying "in a tongue" means uttering words by the direct inspiration of the Holy Spirit — *glossolalia*. These words do not necessarily make sense to the hearers. But " . . . let him who speaks in a tongue pray that he may

---

[8] Claude Tresmontant, *A Study of Hebrew Thought* (New York: Desclée Company, 1960), p. 109.

interpret" (1 Co 14:13). After one has prayed in a tongue, he should explain to his hearers the content of his prayer for their instruction. The spirit here is the "point" of a person which is influenced by the Holy Spirit, and the natural means whereby he prays in this purely supernatural manner. The mind or understanding is a natural faculty, analytic, by which he can make known to others what was given him in his spirit. The spirit, then, is his point of contact with God; the mind, his point of contact with man. In the context, paralleled with the mind, a man's spirit is understood as a faculty, the human faculty for union with God.

In one passage, a first glance gives the impression that Paul believes in Greek trichotomy: "May the God of peace himself sanctify you wholly; and may your spirit and soul and body be kept sound and blameless at the coming of our Lord Jesus Christ" (1 Th 5:23). However, in view of Paul's use of these terms elsewhere, it is evident that he writes as a Hebrew and that these three "elements" of man represent none other than his *ruach, nephesh,* and *bashar. Spirit* here is " . . . that side of the individual being which faces God and the spiritual world, the human spirit which in some sense corresponds to the Spirit of God and is the especial seat of His activity. . . ."[9] We are reminded of the well-known distinction in Hebrews: "For the word of God is living and active, sharper than any two-edged sword, piercing to the division of soul and spirit . . ." (4:12).

Some might question my use of the term *faculty* as applied to the spirit. If the biblical spirit of man is the whole man, body and soul, oriented to and capable of supernatural union with God, doesn't *faculty* imply a part of man? I use it in the same sense that the intellect and will are faculties of the soul. The latter, being spiritual, cannot be divided; the intellect and will are not parts of the soul, but powers; better, they are the soul thinking and willing. In this same sense, then, a man's spirit is his supernatural faculty.[10]

---

[9] Henry Barclay Swete, op. cit., p. 175.
[10] Cf. Phl 3:3–4; 4:23; 1 Tm 3:16; Heb 12:9.

Pneuma can also mean the dominant drive, as can *ruach* in the Old Testament. In this passage we see the *pneuma* as that drive that supernaturalizes the whole conduct: "Did Titus take advantage of you? Have we not walked in the same spirit, have we not walked in the same steps?" (2 Co 12:18).[11]

Union with God can only be accomplished by the spirit. Paul, using sexual union for contrast, is as emphatic as he is terse: "But he who is united to the Lord becomes one spirit with him" (1 Co 6:17). Sexual union is accomplished by means of the body and the result is a new person, as it were — a new *sarx* (6:16; Cf. Eph 5:31). But union with God, achieved by spirit and Spirit, results in a man becoming one with God, without losing his createdness. God is Spirit, outgoing life, and man also is spirit, which causes man to aspire to union with God and seek to obtain that toward which he is directed. As Tresmontant has described this function of the *pneuma*:

> "Man's spirit, his *pneuma*, is that within him which permits an encounter with the *Pneuma* of God. It is the part of a man that can enter into dialogue with God's Spirit, not as a stranger but as a child: 'The Spirit itself bears witness with our spirits that we are children of God' (Rm 8:16)."[12]

I think that the spirit of man as his point of union with God is what the mystics meant by such expressions as the "ground" of the soul or heart, the "spark" or "*scintilla animae*," and the "apex of the soul," etc. Origen, in his Commentary on the Song of Songs, sees the breasts of the Bride " . . . as the ground of the heart in which the Church holds Christ, or the soul holds the Word of God, fast bound and tied to her by the chains of her desire."[13] Mlle. Ancelet-Hustache writes of Meister Eckhart's use of several of these terms:

---

[11] Cf. Rm 2:29; 7:6; 12:11; 1 Co 4:21; 5:5; 2 Co 3:6; 4:13; Gal 6:1, etc.
[12] Claude Tresmontant, op. cit., p. 107.
[13] Origen, *The Song of Songs*, R. P. Lawson, translator (Westminster: The Newman Press, 1957), pp. 165–166.

". . . he sometimes identifies the 'spark of the soul' with the intellect or the superior reason; sometimes he calls it a power, or again he places it well above all the powers. In the same way as the Godhead is 'anterior' to the three Persons according to our way of understanding, so the 'ground' of our soul is that which is 'anterior' to the faculties of the soul. There is an abundance of passages which prove that in Eckhart this 'something,' 'spark,' 'castle' or 'ground' is the basis of all graces of knowledge as well as of love. It is this that receives sanctifying grace and the gifts of the Holy Spirit. It is made in the image of God. This is the imprint of himself that he has left in the soul, where he recognizes himself, and which is capable of receiving him."[14]

Apparently, Eckhart and other mystics who used this terminology, with these concepts, were ignorant of the biblical spirit of man. The *pneuma* is actually what these men were trying to grasp in their complex, dichotomizing, and Greek-influenced thinking. How the *pneuma* was bypassed in the history of Christian spirituality would provide material for another book.[15]

I have already quoted 1 Corinthians 14:14 with reference to the *pneuma* as the supernatural faculty. But something more must be said about the relation of the *pneuma* to the mind, the *nous*, in Paul. Père Reypens has seen the *pneuma* in this passage as

". . . the spirit of man insofar as he is under the action of the Holy Spirit, and as such is distinguished from the simple intellect, *nous*, *mens*. Related to this meaning of *pneuma*, is the distinction between *psychikos* man, who has only natural life, and *pneumatikos* man, who is supernatural, in contact with the Holy Spirit."[16]

As I said above, the mind or intellect or understanding is our natural, analytical, faculty that is our intellectual con-

---

[14] Jeanne Ancelet-Hustache, *Master Eckhart and the Rhineland Mystics* (New York: Harper Torchbooks, 1957), p. 66. Cf. also p. 65. For an example cf. Raymond B. Blakney, *Meister Eckhart* (New York: Harper and Brothers Publishers, 1957), pp. 209–211.

[15] It is interesting to note Father Goldbrunner's references to these terms in relation to the "Self" of C. G. Jung. Cf. Joseph Goldbrunner, *Cure of Mind and Cure of Soul* (New York: Pantheon, 1958), p. 30 n.

[16] L. Reypens, S.J., "Âme," in *Dictionnaire de Spiritualité*, tome I, Col. 435.

tact with the natural. The business man operates daily as a business man by means of his understanding; so does the scientist as a scientist. But when the former relates his workday to God by perceiving the will of God, and works for love of him, he is operating by his *pneuma*. And when the scientist goes to God through his scientific analysis, he does so through his *pneuma*. In the passage from Corinthians the procedure is: God acts on the *pneuma* and the person prays "in a tongue;" then supernaturally enlightened, the understanding breaks down the experience for the benefit of those present. The understanding is essentially the person's perception of the natural.

Paul speaks of "carnal wisdom" (2 Co 1:12), by which he means purely natural wisdom, living by the understanding alone. Or, to put it more concretely, living by such guides as Benjamin Franklin or Dale Carnegie. He condemns the man who is " . . . puffed up by his mere human mind" (literally, the *nous* of the *sarx*) (Col 2:18).

He can seem confusing when he writes of the *pneuma* of the *nous:* "And be renewed in the spirit of your minds, and put on the new nature, created after the likeness of God in true righteousness and holiness" (Eph 4:23). However, this is nothing else than what Prat calls "our supernaturalized intellect,"[17] or our intellect "pneumatized," under the influence of our spirit. An example of the spirit of the mind in action occurs in Colossians when Paul prays " . . . that you may be filled with knowledge of his will, in all spiritual wisdom and understanding" (1:9). It is the supernaturalized intellect that is able to discern what is the will of God here and now, that can rise above pressing daily demands which keep us tending to the horizontal. "Spiritual wisdom and understanding" penetrate to the interior of these demands and find God in his will, and thus the whole is lifted off the humdrum horizontal plane to God.

St. Thomas wrote that man has " . . . a natural aptitude

---

[17] Fernand Prat, S.J., *The Theology of St. Paul* (Westminster: The Newman Bookshop, 1961), vol. II, p. 407.

for understanding and loving God; and this aptitude consists in the very nature of the mind, which is common to all men."[18] While the saint is not writing about the pneuma, but the human intellect, he has grasped the idea of the pneuma of man: "a natural aptitude for understanding and loving God." The texts which we have just been considering explain this aptitude, which does not arise from "the very nature of the mind" as a natural faculty, but from the supernaturalized mind, or the mind impregnated by spirit. The saint says in effect that every man has this aptitude, which is true with regard to the pneuma.

Commenting on Henri de Lubac's *Surnaturel*, Richard Bruch writes that the author

". . . holds for an innate natural desire for the beatific vision; and although this desire is ineffectual, it is nevertheless absolute . . . de Lubac points out that the very desire itself is a free gift of God. The supernatural order in its totality is first in the intention and will of God."[19]

This desire results from the pneuma of man. Since man was created for the beatific vision — made in the image of God, therefore, of his life — this supernatural end is man's formal cause: that which determines his very nature is his supernatural end. And since man is compounded of dust and God's breath, it is this pneuma that keeps man, even though unconsciously, oriented to sharing God's life in the beatific vision.

Tresmontant writes: "The spirit is, within man, a permanent substantial invitation to a change, to a supernaturalization, that will permit created man to partake of his creator's uncreated life."[20]

SPIRIT TO SPIRIT

Among the many meanings Paul attaches to pneuma is that relating it to prophecy. Here Paul brings to fulfillment

---

[18] St. Thomas Aquinas, *Summa Theologica*, I, q. 93, art. 4. The translation is that of the English Dominicans (New York: Benziger Brothers, Inc., 1947).

[19] Richard Bruch, *Theology Digest*, 1960, p. 26.

[20] Claude Tresmontant, op. cit., p. 107.

the Old Testament concept. *Pneuma* as the spirit of prophecy is, I say at the outset, to be distinguished from the *pneuma* of man which we have just been considering. The latter is man's own spirit, an abiding yet supernatural reality. The prophetic spirit is supernatural, charismatic, such as came upon and seized the Old Testament prophets and leaders, and also abode within them as a directive force. As we know from New Testament revelation which we studied in the last chapter, this *ruach* was in reality the Holy Spirit. And with Paul the prophetic *pneuma* of the Christian is the Holy Spirit.

The *ruach* of prophecy was a mediator between God and the prophet: the latter received the word of God only through the mediation of the *ruach*. The Holy Spirit as the *pneuma* of the New Testament prophet — the Christian — is also mediator. He acts upon our *pneuma*, our supernatural faculty, and joins us to Christ: he mediates the Word. "But if anyone does not have the Spirit of Christ, he does not belong to Christ" (Rm 8:9). The Spirit-to-spirit relationship is brought out clearly in Galatians 5:16–25. In verse 16 we read: "Walk in the Spirit, and you will not fulfill the lusts of the flesh." In the next verse Paul switches to the human *pneuma*: "For the flesh lusts against the spirit, and the spirit against the flesh; for these are opposed to each other, so that you do not do what you would." In verse 18 he states that the Holy Spirit is the Christian's power to live by his *pneuma*: "But if you are led by the Spirit, you are not under the Law." He closes the passage by linking union with Christ and the activity of the Spirit: "And they who belong to Christ have crucified their flesh with its passions and desires. If we live by the Spirit, by the Spirit let us also walk" (vv 24–25. Conf. tr.).

In view of these and other Pauline texts which we shall soon consider, we can say that the human *pneuma* is a capacity for the Holy Spirit, who fulfills it. It is in reality a spirit-for-Spirit orientation. And so every human being who is, ever was, and ever will be, is a spirit intended by God to be united with the Holy Spirit. Henry Barclay Swete thus explained this radical orientation:

"The Holy Spirit does not create the 'spirit' in man; it is potentially present in every man, even if rudimentary and undeveloped. Every human being has affinities with the spiritual and eternal. In each individual of the race *the spirit of the man which is in him* (1 Cor 2:11) answers to the Spirit of God, in so far as the finite can correspond with the infinite; though there are men who are psychic and not spiritual, who may even be said not to 'have spirit' (Jude 19), human nature is incomplete without it, and vainly seeks satisfaction in sensual or even in intellectual enjoyment (Eph 4:17 ff). But though the Spirit of God finds in man a spiritual nature on which it can work, the human spirit is in so imperfect or depraved a condition that a complete renovation, even a re-creation, is necessary (2 Cor 5:17).[21]

This new creation is the work of the Holy Spirit: "Did you receive the Spirit by works of the law, or by hearing with faith? Are you so foolish? Having begun in the Spirit, are you now ending with the flesh?" (Gal 3:2–3); "But we are bound to give thanks to God always for you, brethren beloved by the Lord, because God chose you from the beginning to be saved through sanctification by the Spirit and belief in the truth" (2 Th 2:13); "And such were some of you. But you were washed, you were sanctified, you were justified in the name of our Lord Jesus Christ and in the Spirit of our God" (1 Co 6:11). This new creation is man as Christ. The first creation is Adamic man, and although he is created in the image of God, and oriented to God by reason of his *ruach*, Adamic man is incomplete in himself because he is unfulfilled. The complete image of God is Christ — the life of God in Christ — and the spirit of man drives him toward his fulfillment as Christ. Commenting on this passage " . . . Adam, who is a figure of him who was to come" (Rm 5:14), Karl Barth writes:

"The relationship between Adam and us reveals not the primary but only the secondary anthropological truth and ordering principle. The primary anthropological truth and ordering prin-

---

[21] Henry Barclay Swete, op. cit., p. 342.

ciple, which only mirrors itself in that relationship, is made clear only through the relationship between Christ and us. . . . Man's essential and original nature is to be found, therefore, not in Adam but in Christ. In Adam we can only find it pre-figured. Adam can therefore be interpreted only in the light of Christ and not the other way round."[22]

Adam is the father of our *sarx*, of our natural life; Christ, the second Adam, as "a life-giving spirit [*pneuma*]" (1 Co 15:45), which is the life of God, is the source of the true life of our *pneuma*, the life of God that is in him, and the Holy Spirit mediates that life: " . . . the Spirit of the life in Christ Jesus . . ." (Rm 8:2).

Man is fulfilled as Christ by his union with Christ's body, and this union is the work of the Holy Spirit: "For by one Spirit we were all baptized into one body, Jews or Greeks, slaves or free — and all were made to drink of one Spirit" (1 Co 12:13); " . . . eager to maintain the unity of the Spirit in the bond of peace. There is one body and one Spirit, just as you were called to the one hope that belongs to your call, one Lord, one faith, one baptism, one God and Father of all, who is above all, and through all and in all" (Eph 4:3-6). Paul also uses the metaphor of a building to express the union of Christians with Christ, which building is con-structed by the Holy Spirit: "In whom [Christ] you also are built into it for a dwelling place of God in the Spirit" (Eph 2:22). The Spirit accomplishes this union through baptism: " . . . he saved us through the bath of regeneration and renewal by the Holy Spirit; whom he has abundantly poured out upon us through Jesus Christ our Savior" (Tt 3:5-6).

The result of the union of Christ's body with himself as its head is one person: "For you are all one [person] in Christ Jesus" (Gal 3:28). The Greek word for "one" here is in the masculine, not the neuter, and means, therefore, not one thing or mere entity, but one man, or person.[23] Thus is man fulfilled as man: he is united, spirit to Spirit,

---

[22] Karl Barth, *Christ and Adam* (New York: Collier Books, 1962), pp. 39–40.

[23] Cf. Émile Mersch, S.J., *The Whole Christ* (Milwaukee: The Bruce Publishing Company, 1938), p. 135.

in Christ. And the Spirit remains in him, as in Christ's human nature, as the principle and source of his supernatural activity: "But you are not in the flesh, you are in the Spirit, if the Spirit of God really dwells in you. Any one who does not have the Spirit of Christ does not belong to him" (Rm 8:9).

But the person to whom the body is united is that of God the Son, hence the parts of the body become adopted children of the Father. United to the Son by the Spirit, Christians live out their adopted sonship by the same Spirit: "For all who are led by the Spirit of God are sons of God. For you did not receive the spirit of slavery to fall back into fear, but you have received a spirit of sonship. When we cry, 'Abba! Father!' it is the Spirit himself bearing witness with our spirit that we are children of God" (Rm 8:14–16).

But in Galatians Paul says that it is the Spirit himself who cries: "Abba!" within us: "And because you are sons, God has sent the Spirit of his Son into our hearts, crying, 'Abba, Father' " (Gal 4:6). It is the same Spirit which enabled the human nature of Christ while on earth to say "Abba!" so lovingly and constantly to the Father. The Spirit of Christ is our Spirit, enabling us, the extension and continuation of Christ, to be oriented to the Father in the Father-centered religion of Christ. He is "the Spirit of the life in Christ Jesus" (Rm 8:2). In other words, the Spirit is the life of Christ's body, in the sense that that body lives a supernatural life. The Holy Spirit is the life of Father and Son, for he is their love, and this is their eternal act — their mutual self-giving life that is nothing else but love. God is spirit insofar as he is dynamic, outgoing life, or love. And the Holy Spirit is the life of Christ's body because that life has to be one eternal act — love, and he is that love: " . . . the love of God is poured forth in our hearts by the Holy Spirit who has been given to us" (Rm 5:5). To repeat: the life of God is love, the personalized act of love who is the Holy Spirit; the life of the body of Christ, the extension of the incarnate Son, is love, the Holy Spirit. The Father is loving the Son in his body by means of the Spirit, and by that same Spirit the whole Christ is loving the Father.

Prayer is the loving communication of the Son with the Father, and in his body it is the Spirit who maintains this communication. Paul tells the Ephesians: "pray at all times in the Spirit, with all prayer and supplication . . ." (6:18). It is true that the Holy Spirit prays for us: "Likewise the Spirit helps us in our weakness; for we do not know how to pray as we ought, but the Spirit himself intercedes for us with sighs too deep for words. And he who searches the hearts of men knows what is the mind of the Spirit, because the Spirit intercedes for the saints according to the will of God" (Rm 8:26–27). But his prayer is more than just praying for us: we cannot pray, nor do any supernatural act, except in him, in his act: "And no one can say 'Jesus is Lord,' except by the Holy Spirit" (1 Co 12:3).

But the end of his activity in the body of Christ is something more than mere communication and means; it is something definite and ultimate — the formation of Christ in each one in the body, or rather, the formation of each one into Christ: "And we all, with unveiled face, beholding the glory of the Lord, are being changed into his likeness from one degree of glory to another; for this comes from the Lord who is the Spirit" (2 Co 3:18).

So we come to the end, the purpose, of the human *pneuma*: to be acted on by the Holy Spirit, the *Hagion Pneuma*, who makes us into Christ. The *pneuma* as man, capable of and oriented to this supernatural destiny, is completed by the Spirit, as a man is fulfilled by becoming Christ.[24]

---

[24] Paul can also use *spirit* to mean something strictly supernatural, such as the grace of adoption: Rm 8:15; special supernatural gifts: 1 Co 12:1–11; 14:1; grace: Gal 4:29. His use of *pneumatikos*, "spiritual" (which among the New Testament writers is peculiar to him, except for one exception, 1 Pt 2:5), has this supernatural sense. Cf. Gal 6:1; 1 Co 15:44–46; Eph 1:3; 5:19; Col 1:9. Here, then, the term means God's life, his creative power, shared with man by means of his Spirit. Cf. Karl Rahner, S.J., *Theological Investigations* (Baltimore: Helicon Press, 1961), vol. I, pp. 320–322.

CHAPTER 8

The Spirit of Man
in the New Testament:
The Life of God

John completes the biblical doctrine of man, and does so with the unction that characterizes him. "God is spirit [pneuma]" (Jn 4:24), he tells us, and "God is love" (1 Jn 4:8), thus giving us the real meaning of pneuma, the truth, the reality of which the pneuma of man is nothing but a Platonic shadow. When Jesus says to Nicodemus: " . . . that which is born of the Spirit is spirit" (Jn 3:6), he is saying that the Christian life consists of love, that this love is purely supernatural, and that it is the gift of him who is Love in the Trinity. In other words, he is saying that the life of God becomes the life of the Christian.

Life is one of the major themes of John's Gospel. In fact, his account of Christ's public life, Chapters 2–12, is mainly a collection of events, speeches, and dialogues bearing on the theme of eternal life. It is John who reveals the purpose of the incarnation and redemption: "I came that they may have life, and have it abundantly" (Jn 10:10).

How are we to receive that life? "Truly, truly, I say to you, unless one is born of water and the Spirit, he cannot enter the kingdom of God" (Jn 3:5). Baptism by water and the Spirit, foretold by John the Baptist (Jn 1:33), confers the everlasting life that is in Christ. This is a rebirth. Birth is the beginning of life in the actual human situation; it can even be considered a creation in the sense that the newborn is now apparent to the senses, and thus is known to be.

In the Old Testament creation, especially the creation of man, is ascribed to the Spirit of God. Man exists as himself, a living *nephesh*, because of God's breath (Gn 2:7). We have only to re-read the texts given in Chapter 4 and more particularly to recall the *ruach* of God hovering over the waters about to create, in order to be convinced of the connection of the Spirit and creation. Re-creation in the moral order is also the work of the Spirit — Ezekiel's vision of the Spirit and the dry bones comes to mind. Hence the re-creation that results from baptism is ascribed to the Spirit: born again of the Spirit — baptism with the Spirit. The new life for the moral order is his work.

"Born again" in John 3:5 can as well be translated "born from above," for the Greek adverb *anothen* has both meanings. "From above" relates to the Spirit, and fits in well with the following verse: "That which is born of the flesh is flesh, and that which is born of the Spirit is spirit." The first birth of the Christian is, according to the flesh, *kata sarka*, placing him on the horizontal plane of natural living. The second birth is "from above," by the Spirit, from God. Strictly supernatural, it puts him into the order of supernatural living. As such it is clearly a rebirth, as Nicodemus, to whom Jesus' words were addressed, understood it.[1]

The apostles were born again on Easter night when Christ " . . . breathed on them, and said to them, 'Receive the Holy Spirit' " (Jn 20:22). This was their re-creation as Christians, by an action that paralleled the first creation of man by God's breath and thus not only indicated a new creation but also attributed it to the Spirit.

The apostles' baptism was the first in the Church, their rebirth the first into the new life in Christ. Creation and re-creation, birth and rebirth are acts of the Spirit, because the Spirit gives life. "It is the Spirit that gives life" says Christ, and he equates the two in the same context (Jn

---

[1] Cf. C. K. Barrett, *The Gospel according to St. John* (London: S.P.C.K., 1962), pp. 171–172. The relation of water and life in the Old Testament goes without saying; e.g., the water from the rock in Ex 17:1–6, and Nm 20:2–11. Cf. also Je 2:13; Is 58:11; Ezk 47:1–12.

6:63).[2] Christ's object is to give life, and he does so initially
in the rebirth of baptism by the Spirit.

When Christ tells the Samaritan woman: "God is
spirit . . ." (Jn 4:24), he gives us an insight into the life
of God that makes us realize why that life is trinitarian.
In Chapter 4 I said that the term ruach in the Old Testament reveals much about God's being: first of all, it tells
us that God is act, that he is dynamic rather than static.
It also tells us that God is creative and life-giving power;
that he is love, for his power-acts in creation are on behalf
of his creation: life, protection, sustenance, his saving word
to his beloved people. All of the acts of God by his ruach on
behalf of the Israelites are motivated by and concretely
demonstrate his love. We can say that his ruach is his own
personal life flowing outside of himself, his life outgoing to
create and to love what he has created.

Thus in the New Testament, when Jesus declares in John's
Gospel, "God is spirit," John means all of this, as his Jewish
readers would readily understand, and more. In the context
of his Gospel, the passages revealing the true life of God, the
Trinity, we see that pneuma as God means first the act, the
outgoing life, the love of God that is directed to God: "but I
do as the Father has commanded me, so that the world may
know that I love the Father . . ." (Jn 14:31); "As the Father
has loved me, so have I loved you. . . . If you keep my commandments, you will abide in my love, just as I have kept
my Father's commandments and abide in his love" (Jn
15:9–10); "I glorified thee on earth, having accomplished
the work which thou gavest me to do; and now, Father,
glorify thou me in thy own presence with the glory which
I had with thee before the world was made" (Jn 17:4–5).
These are a few of the trinitarian texts in John, but they
reveal God as Father and Son loving each other by a love

[2] I capitalize the "S" of spirit because it is obviously the Holy Spirit, in
agreement with the biblical idea of the Spirit of God as giver of life. Cf.
C. K. Barrett, op. cit., p. 251; Lindsay Dewar, The Holy Spirit and Modern
Thought (New York: Harper and Brothers Publishers, 1960), p. 185; Ray-
mond E. Brown, S.S., The Gospel of St. John and the Johannine Epistles
(Collegeville: The Liturgical Press, 1960), p. 42.

that is dynamic, effective, carried out by the human acts of Christ. They reveal the life of God as love of God. *Pneuma* as God is outgoing: the Father giving his being to the Son, and the Son giving himself to the Father. *Pneuma*, then, is "creative" in that the Father is the source of being for the Son.

John elsewhere says that God is Love (1 Jn 4:8), but we know from his Gospel that this love is trinitarian in its radical meaning. The important thing is that he not only equates spirit with life, but also spirit with love. I shall return to this, and the consequent equation of life with love, which runs through the first and second Johannine epistles.

When Jesus tells Nicodemus that " . . . that which is born of the Spirit is spirit" (Jn 3:6), he is telling us that the Spirit is the source of the Christian life, which is love. The designation *Spirit* for the revealed third Person of the Trinity would convey to the Christian convert from Judaism the creative, dynamic love of God. But in the light of the trinitarian revelation in John's Gospel and first Epistle, the convert would conclude that this Spirit is also, and basically, the love of Father and Son for each other. Hence, the Spirit abiding in the Christian is not so much God loving him, but God in him loving God.[3] What is born of this abiding Spirit is the life of God given to the Christian: it is the dynamic outgoing power of love, directed to God, and to God in our brothers. This, then, is John's concept of the spirit of man. He presumes the human spirit. As a Jew, he is well-acquainted with the Old Testament *ruach*.[4] But there is no need in his plan to mention it specifically as such, except in 3:6 of his Gospel, where he sees it in its fulfillment. Man's basic orientation to union with God is completed and satisfied by the very life of God given to him by the Spirit of God. This is readily understood from the first part of the verse: "That which is born of the flesh is flesh." John knows *sarx* as mere human nature, good in itself, but still on the natural level.

---

[3] Cf. 1 Jn 3:24; 4:13.
[4] Cf. John's references to the *pneuma* as wind: Jn 3:8; seat of emotions: Jn 11:33; 13:21.

Man comes alive as a complete human person, as *pneuma*, at his rebirth.[5]

What about Christ's use of spirit in his dialogue with the Samaritan woman — "in spirit and in truth?" As in 3:6, it derives its precise meaning from its relation to the same word used in reference to God in the immediate context: "That which is born of the Spirit is spirit" (3:6), "God is spirit, and those who worship him must worship in spirit and in truth" (Jn 4:24. Cf. verse 23). In either case the second spirit is a result of the first. "God is spirit" means, as we have seen, the outgoing life of God that is love — the love of Father and Son for each other by means of the Spirit, and for man by the gift of the same Spirit. Therefore, God must be worshipped "in spirit," that is, by the same outgoing life that is love, which is the gift of the Spirit in the rebirth of baptism. C. H. Dodd says that spirit and truth in this passage are a "virtual hendiadys."[6] This is so because truth here means the reality of God's life — that life as it is. To worship God in spirit and in truth means, then, to know, love, and acknowledge his divinity as he does. Here is that life of God for which the spirit of man is a capacity, for which God's breath is in him turning him Godward.[7]

John truly crowns the biblical doctrine of the spirit of man. He has given us the completed teaching of revelation. I think he has done this best in 3:6: "That which is born of the flesh is flesh; and that which is born of the Spirit is spirit." The spirit of man is, for the Christian, the spirit of God that is God's life. Flesh, the natural level, is incapable

---

[5] *Flesh* in Jn 6:63 refers to Christ's flesh, mentioned in vv. 53–57. His human nature by itself is nothing. It is the divine nature, given to it by the Spirit at his incarnation, that gives it value. Cf. C. K. Barrett, op. cit., p. 251.

[6] C. H. Dodd, *The Interpretation of the Fourth Gospel* (Cambridge: University Press, 1963), p. 224.

[7] A related meaning of *pneuma* in vv. 23–24 can be seen from vv. 20–21. Worshipping God in a definite place, e.g., Jerusalem has a "sarkical" tone: *sarx* is man as "locatable" in space, the *ubi* and *situs* of Aristotle's categories. It would almost seem as if God is only "locatable" at Jerusalem, hence the worshipper has to be "locatable" there, too. The *pneuma* is not confined to space, but is the person as outgoing. Paul says the same thing in 1 Co 3:5–4, and Col 2:5 — absent in the *sarx*, which is confined to a definite place, but present in the outgoing *pneuma*.

of this divine, trinitarian life. The human spirit, while a faculty for living by this life, is of itself powerless to do so. It is activated, made capable, by "spirit," the gift of God's life by the Spirit. This spirit is in reality a participation in the Spirit; it is God in man choosing himself. Or, to put it another way, this supernatural spirit is by its nature God, just as the sun rays in a room are by their nature the sun. It is what theology calls sanctifying grace — the life of God who is spirit. It is what theologians term "uncreated grace," the indwelling Spirit. Man was created in God's image, then, because God gave him his *ruach*, which God is.[8]

However, there are still several important points in John's Gospel that have to be considered before we can fully grasp his complete teaching on the spirit. First we should look at his way of treating our knowledge of God. Christ's purpose is to give life (10:10; 20:31). But in his prayer to the Father he states that this life consists of knowing God: "This is eternal life, that they know thee the only true God, and Jesus Christ whom thou hast sent" (17:3). Just what is this knowledge? Is it something purely intellectual, the recognition of the truth of God? No. Rather is this knowledge like that of Adam knowing his wife, and thereby conceiving a son (Gn 4:1) — the experience of another. When two friends know each other they indeed know the truth about each other, but their knowledge results from intimate experience, from living a good deal of the time together, not from intellectual analysis. This is the way Jesus uses "knowledge": "I am the good shepherd, and I know mine and mine know me, even as the Father knows me and I know the Father . . ." (Jn 10:14–15). Geerhardus Vos has made a good distinction:

> "It is true, the Gospel teaches that to know God is life eternal. But the concept of 'knowledge' here is not to be understood in its Hellenic sense, but in the Semitic sense. According to the former 'to know' means to mirror the reality of a thing in one's consciousness. The Semitic and biblical idea is to have

---

8 I am indebted to my former student, G. P. Williams, for several of these insights.

the reality of something practically interwoven with the inner experience of life. Hence, 'to know' can stand in the Biblical idiom for 'to love,' 'to single out in love'. . . . The circle of revelation is not a school, but a 'covenant.' "[9]

In his discourse after the Last Supper Christ tells the Apostles: "And I will pray the Father, and he will give you another Counselor, to be with you for ever, even the Spirit of truth, whom the world cannot receive, because it neither sees him nor knows him; you know him, for he dwells with you, and will be in you" (Jn 14:16–17). The expression "Spirit of truth," which also occurs elsewhere in John (15:26; 16:13) means, according to C. K. Barrett: "The Spirit who communicates truth, who himself is directly acquainted with all truth and imparts truth to all who receive him."[10] The truth which the Spirit communicates is the reality of God, the "truth about God," i.e., his trinitarian life. The Christian knows this truth in experiencing the Spirit dwelling within him. Thus his knowledge departs from the purely intellectual into the dynamic, for he is intimately experiencing the Love of God.

The trinitarian mode of the Christian life is the last important point in John that we shall consider in relation to the spirit. I would be bold enough to call this life a "circuminsession"; the words of Christ permit no other expression. For example, in his prayer to the Father: " . . . that they may be one even as we are one" (Jn 17:11), "that they may all be one; even as thou, Father, art in me, and I in thee, that they also may be in us . . ." (17:21). These words do not indicate mere Christian unity, but the mode of that unity, as the following verses clearly state: "The glory which thou hast given me, I have given to them, that they may be one even as we are one, I in them and thou in me, that they may become perfectly one, so that the world may know that thou hast sent me and hast loved them even as thou hast

[9] Geerhardus Vos, *Biblical Theology* (Grand Rapids: Wm. B. Eerdmans Publishing Company, 1963), p. 17.

[10] C. K. Barrett, "The Holy Spirit in the Fourth Gospel," *Journal of Theological Studies*, vol. I (new series), 1950, p. 8.

loved me" (Jn 17:22–23). The unity is accomplished in
Christ: "I in them." The Father sees and loves the Son as
the whole Christ — Paul's body of Christ: " . . . that the love
with which thou hast loved me may be in them, and I in
them" (17:26). The Christian enters the Trinity in Christ,
yet remains a creature: "No one comes to the Father but
through me" (Jn 14:6); " . . . I am in my Father, and you
in me, and I in you" (Jn 14:20). The Christian life is thus
understood as a "circuminsession."

The thing to note here, however, is that the Christian is
in Christ, in him as God and man. The union is organic,
John 15 emphasizes; the vine and branches are not a metaphor but a symbol signifying a union that is based on the
sharing of life.[11] It is, again, that of "circuminsession" —
"Abide in me, and I in you" (15:4). Christ is more specific
in his discourse on the bread of life or Eucharist: "He who
eats my flesh and drinks my blood abides in me, and I in
him. As the living Father sent me, and I live because of the
Father, so he who eats me will live because of me" (Jn
6:56–57). The life which Christ has come to give is actually
that which is in *him*, which those who are united in him share
and live by. The Christian life is Christ's life.

The Spirit is the immediate source of this life: " 'If any
one thirst, let him come to me and drink. He who believes
in me, as the scripture has said, Out of his heart shall flow
rivers of living water.' Now this he said about the Spirit,
which those who believed in him were to receive; for as yet
the Spirit had not been given, because Jesus was not yet
glorified" (Jn 7:37–39). This is the water of which Christ
speaks to the Samaritan woman: " . . . the water that I will
give him shall become in him a fountain of water, springing
up unto life everlasting" (Jn 4:14). The Spirit gives this
life initially in baptism, and abides within the person as a
continual source.

Christ is the meriting source of the Spirit, basically through
his death, at which moment he " . . . gave up his spirit"

---

[11] Cf. C. H. Dodd, *op. cit.*, pp. 136–140.

(Jn 19:30). The Greek verb (*paradidomi*) means rather that Christ handed over, entrusted, his Spirit. And in view of the three witnesses to Christ in 1 John 5:8 — the Spirit, the water, and the blood — this Spirit is in reality the Holy Spirit which Christ gives to the Church in the sacraments of baptism and Eucharist.[12] The thing to note is that Christ gives the Spirit that is in *him*, whom Paul calls "the Spirit of Christ" (Rm 8:9), and "the Spirit of the life in Christ Jesus" (Rm 8:2). The Spirit is in Christ as the divine life of love of the Son for the Father, and it is the Spirit in Christ who is in the Christian, leading him to love as an adopted son (Rm 8:14).[13] God is Spirit — outgoing, creative love — and the Spirit is God, the personification of that love. For the Christian, he abides in him, already abiding in Christ, creating Christ in him anew.

So, although John does not mention the spirit of man as such, he envisions it as fulfilled, realized, by the Spirit. Simply, with few words, by a clear synthesis, he delineates man as destined for the life of the Trinity, in the Son. The real meaning of God's breath in man has been completely revealed.

---

[12] Cf. David Stanley, S.J., "The New Testament Doctrine of Baptism," *Theological Studies* (June, 1957), p. 204.

[13] For adoption in John cf. Jn 1:12–13; 1 Jn 3:2.

CHAPTER 9

Conclusions:
The "Spiritual" Life

We have reached the chapter for which I have written the preceding. It is at this point that the reader who has persevered thus far has one large question: "How can biblical man live today?" Which is to say, how can I, with my body, my intellect and will, emotions, temperament, background, education, family, work, obligations, to say nothing of neuroses, live as the biblical man I actually am? How do I do it? This chapter, then, and that following, are the practical corollaries of the biblical doctrine — this chapter in particular, because it is a summing-up of the three aspects of biblical man, and a general conclusion as to what to do.

Synthesis

By now we may have lost sight of the woods because of a detailed attention to the trees. Hence a summary and a synthesis of the chapters on man as flesh, soul, and spirit is necessary here.

Man is a unity of flesh, soul, and spirit. I do not say a composite, because that term connotes unification, a "making one," of elements that do not essentially belong together. A unification is not per se one, but only accidentally. A school, for example, is essentially a unity of teachers and pupils. The addition of coaches and hot-lunch people would make the resultant whole a unification, not a unity, because these latter are accidental to a school qua school. Greek man as he has emerged from the hands of St. Thomas is a unity, even though he is two quite different substances. The reason is that in man these two substances *belong* together, as matter and form. Biblical man, however, is not two, or three, substances but a simple unity.

It is easy for one who has not carefully studied biblical man to conclude that he and scholastic man are one and the same, that, after all, flesh is the body, biblical soul is in reality scholastic soul, and spirit, the supernaturalization of the two. While he would be correct on the last conclusion, not so on the former. Flesh and biblical soul are wider concepts: they are not coextensive with body and soul.

Although biblical man is seen as *sarx-psychē-pneuma*, there is a twofold distinction. The scholastics, and all who follow the Greeks, would say it is between body and soul. The biblical writers, if they would distinguish at all, have it between *sarx-psychē* and *pneuma*, that is, between flesh-soul on the one hand, and spirit on the other. The basis for distinction is not that of matter and non-matter, or matter and form, but that of natural and supernatural. The distinction is not of substances or causality, but of orders. To restate: the Western mind analyzes, the biblical mind relates. The latter does not need to synthesize because it never sees a thing detached from essential relationship. The biblical mind, therefore, sees man, not as divided, but as related, and there are two relationships: God and nature.

In order to see this viewpoint better, we must go back and review the meanings of *sarx*, *psychē*, and *pneuma*. We have seen that *sarx* stands for the bodily material of man, his flesh, or "flesh-meat." It can thus mean the body, but never what we mean by body — a neat composite of orderly systems. For the biblical writers the body (*sōma* in the New Testament) is the person as exterior — not a part, nor an outer shell for this view would be divisive, but the unity as related to others, persons as well as things. Hence *sarx* can be kinship, and it can denote the whole man too. Since it expresses a relationship to creation — because *sarx* is perceptible and hence designates the human person as immediately knowable — and, more deeply, since *sarx* is what all creatures of earth have in common, it places man on the horizontal plane of earthly creation. Here he is in opposition to God, who is not *sarx*, but *pneuma*. The New Testament takes this last point further, particularly Paul who, stressing the redemptive work of Christ, sees *sarx* as it is because of Adam's sin — weak, and in itself tending to sin. In the main *sarx* means the whole man considered as a natural human being related to this earth and its creatures. For those who have read Harvey Cox's *The Secular City*, such a person should "ring a bell." But more of this in the next chapter. However, man as *sarx* is definitely Renaissance man — divorced from God for all practical purposes, and very much alive in the here and now. Although *sarx* has been so often translated by "flesh," its meanings definitely exclude the body considered *in se*, and unrelated. I cannot insist too strongly on this. Biblical "flesh" is always *ad alios et alia*.

Psychē is the whole of *sarx* considered as living. This might be a bit off the truth, but it would be helpful to imagine *sarx* as a person in a tableau, in which he is seen in definite relation to other persons and objects, a static conception. Now see the tableau suddenly transformed into a play: the characters come alive and our man begins to move and live out his relationships. This is what *psychē* does to *sarx*: it makes it come alive and start to act. The concept, therefore, that *psychē* conveys is that of life.

Because *psychē* is the person as living, it more truly denotes the person, and thus is considered to be the personality itself, the origin of appetites and emotions, of thinking and willing. These human functions are assigned to bodily organs, it is true, but they act only because of the *psychē*, because the *sarx* is alive and therefore active. The living person is the responsible person, hence the latter is also the *psychē*: the word with a possessive adjective intensifies the pronoun — "his *psychē*" is "himself."

But *psychē* is life relative to the person. This is what *makes* the person. Therefore it is almost ridiculous to say that it is natural to man, since without *psychē* we do not have man.

Still, it must be said, because the psyche makes sarx to be simple, natural man, it places him among God's creatures. It does nothing more than this. It puts this perceptible, "locatable," creation in action with his fellow creatures, but never gets him "off the ground." Psyche, like sarx, equips man for "gracious horizontal living." It is relative, true, but to this particular sarx, which then is capable of going out to others. Psyche makes natural man, stands for natural man, and leaves him natural.

Psyche is therefore the whole person as alive. Basically it is inseparable from the sarx, or "unseparatable." Even when belief in an after-life forces the Hebrews to accept some kind of a disembodied psyche, it is not quite divested of the sarx, for it has a form as in life, and at least is sarx insofar as it is a human creature. And here is the radical basis for the theological conclusion that there must be a resurrection of the body, at least for the just. The revealed fact of Christ's resurrection is the assurance that this conclusion was inspired.

But psyche can only produce Renaissance man, working and scheming for self, and for humanity at best, a settled citizen of the secular city. However, the word "produce" jars the reader who knows his biblical man. Actually the psyche produces nothing, but is itself produced. Man becomes a living psyche only because of God's breath. To ignore or disbelieve in this vital breath would be to accept the caused as cause, and, moreover, to be ignorant of the essential relation to God which his breath has made.

There is all the difference in the world in saying simply that God made man and the statement in Genesis 2:7. God formed dust and breathed into it the breath of life, and thus man became a living being, a psyche. In all the rest of the creation account God merely speaks and it is made. The writer states the revealed difference with regard to man: he is man, he exists as a human being, because there is something of God in him which begins him, and keeps him bound to God as a preserver and as a directing force. Man is religious by the mere fact of his existence. Even if God had created him as he had the rest, by simple volition, man would still have to seek him and his will. But what the Genesis account is saying is that man in his reality as man is a Godward dimension that can only be fulfilled by God, that by his very nature he is an orientation to God that leaves him with no other choice. He is free to choose God, but if he doesn't, he frustrates his nature of human being. This meaning is borne out by parallel texts which we have already studied.

Thus to say that man is body and soul is correct as far as it goes, but is an incomplete statement. Even though we repudiate the Platonic notion of the supremacy of the soul with the body as its prison, and adhere to the vital, essential, union of the two, we are right philosophically, but not biblically. Body and soul do not in themselves imply a supernatural direction to man, and certainly not a supernaturalization. They indicate simply natural man, who, in the light of the Bible, does not actually exist. The spirit of man — God's breath — means that this human life — body and soul, if you like — is necessarily directed to God, and is completed by the Spirit with his gift of the divine life. God's breath in man gives the lie to Renaissance man, to the supremacy of man, and to the validity of mere humanitarianism. Because of it nothing that is human can be viewed apart from God, whether in one's personal life, or in, for example, a discipline such as sociology. God's breath in man changes the way we regard man, and the way he regards the universe.

I have said that the distinction is between *sarx-psychē* and *pneuma*, between man as natural and supernatural. How does *pneuma* relate to and interact with the other two aspects of man? We must remember that *pneuma* is, like the *psychē*, life; and there are not two different lives but the same life. *Psychē* is human life in itself; *pneuma*, however, indicates the true nature of this life — it is God's breath. *Pneuma* penetrates deeper than does *psychē*, which doesn't say enough. The case is something like *ball game* not being as informative as *baseball game*. The truth about *psychē*, then, is that it is really *pneuma*, God's breath in man, the source of his life as well as the life itself. Thus both are coextensive, and it is easy to see why, as time went on, they could be used interchangeably. The Hebrew knew the difference, just as we know that when someone speaks about a ball game during the summer, he means baseball. *Pneuma* is human life received from God and directed to him, or life related to God, as *psychē* is life related to the person.

Is the pneuma the whole *person*? Does it include the *sarx*? Yes, insofar as the *psychē* includes the whole person. *Sarx*, as we have seen, is the visible, perceptible *psychē*. When we see the *sarx* in motion, we are looking at the *psychē*, not merely at a moving hand or leg, but at the life of a person concentrated at the moment in that member. But this life is in reality God's breath, this is the person's life force, and so we are actually beholding his *pneuma*. In this sense, then, is the *pneuma* the whole man.

How, then, can we even distinguish the natural and supernatural in man? We can only see different aspects, not separate realities, and thus are we able to make a distinction. But we cannot make a clear-cut division: here is natural man, *sarx-psychē*, and here is what gives him a supernatural orientation, the *pneuma*; because while it is true that the *pneuma* does create this orientation, it also causes natural man. Hence, although the Bible does not line up the "material" *sarx* against the "spiritual" *psychē* and *pneuma*, neither does it conceive of man in the state of pure nature who becomes supernaturalized. If man is de *facto* elevated to the supernatural level by sanctifying grace, he was destined for it by his very creation as man. It is man who makes the distinction, falsely, and chooses to live in the "flesh," on the purely natural level. Existentially his position is as false as that of the person who chooses to live like a dog. He can certainly do so, but he's missing the point of life.

The human soul is not synonymous with spirit in the Bible, even in the New Testament. If there is a development at all, it is rather one of language — employing the terminology of apocalyptic. Hence Paul's flesh lusting against the spirit is not the body lusting against the soul, but the *sarx-psyché* opposing the *pneuma* because of their different orders. *Pneuma*, spirit, to the Hebrew of Old and New Testaments conveyed, at least unconciously, the life of man as related to God, particularly to the Spirit of God. The soul, separable after all, is still, in that state, not the detached soul of the philosophers, but rather a warm, human thing, or more properly, person, invested with the humanness of the *sarx*, from which it cannot quite be separated. And considered as spirit, this *psyché* is divine in its origin and its end, and, for the person in grace, in its elevation. Any other "soul" is hypothetical, because it's divorced from the fullness with which revelation has endowed it.

LIVING WHOLLY

In view of the biblical doctrine of man such an expression as "the spiritual life" needs qualification. If it means the life of the soul with a minimizing of that of the body, it does not express biblical, and certainly not Christian life. Biblical man is a unified whole; thus the Christian life is integral living. The spiritual life means, then, the proper, unified life of *sarx*, *psyché* and *pneuma*-of the whole person.

Christian living, therefore, does not deny the body. By this I do not exclude self-denial, as that term is understood in the history of our spirituality. I am rather referring to an attitude which we can call "angelism," an attitude that deplores the body's existence and union with the soul at all, and regards the Christian life as one in which the needs and healthy rights of the body are denied as far as "inhumanly possible." These needs and rights are regarded as inimical to the Christian life of the soul, the only true life of the person. The end result is to live as much like an angel — a disembodied soul — as possible. That such a way of life is necessary for certain rare people I grant. But this is not the norm nor the ideal.

Such a mentality is not so common, and it is easy to combat when it arises. Far more common with spiritual writers, and

I include influential writers from past centuries, is the feeling that the body is practically the sole source of sin. Their use of "flesh" is no more vituperative than Paul's, but they don't mean the same thing he does — they mean the body, weakened by reason of original sin, but nothing more than the body. They decry the sensual, the carnal, and while they don't go as far as the "angelists" in complete body-denial, they leave one with a pessimistic attitude toward the body that condemns it before it has even done anything. I might call these writers facetiously the two-strikes-on-the-body group.

More common still, and quite subtle, are those who speak of "the life of the soul," and forget about the body. These are more elevated in their matter and approach, appealing to the advanced, to whom "sins of the flesh" would be in rather poor taste. They refer to the person as "the soul." Christ did this, too, it might be objected, in a parable about a rich farmer who addressed himself: "Soul, thou hast many good things laid up for many years . . ." (Lk 12:19; Kleist tr.). The word here is *psychē*, which means more than these writers' "souls." The inference is that the soul is the only important component of man, and once the grosser sins have been eliminated, it is free to soar and develop by grace to union with God. The body is there, of course, much as the neglected spouses of certain public persons are there — affable, self-effacing, and handy. But not very necessary. Thus the body is ignored, a far more devastating fate than if it were hotly railed against. Devotees of this school, the "spirituals," would find a real, tangible union of their bodies with the body of Christ in the Eucharist and in the Mystical Body — which is really not so mystical — distasteful, because "carnal," if they thought about it. I really don't think they know about such a union, because it would hardly be considered necessary: after all the union is "spiritual."

One mistake all of these persons make is in creating a basic distinction — if not division — between "matter and spirit" in man. (It would be better if the distinction were between "man as matter and non-matter.") The biblical attitude is toward man regarded as natural and supernatural — one of differing orders, not elements. Writers such as those mentioned here either have been ignorant of, or have ignored, spirit, pneuma, as the supernatural aspect, and have failed to recognize in practice the fundamental unity of body and soul, absolutely necessary for human nature.

The Christian man must, because he is Christian, live wholly, that is, by body and soul together. His unity is a revealed fact, to which the man of the philosophers must yield and adapt. Hence the spiritual life is quite a corporal affair, and has to be. It may involve the theater, followed by a drink and a welsh rarebit, or a round of golf, as well as the infused prayer of quiet and the Dark Night of the Senses. Probably the latter would thrive better for being the context of the former.

The emotions provide an excellent example of living wholly, for they are definitely psychophysical. We are well aware of biblical man's pneuma swelling up in anger, or fainting away from fear; we know of the desires of the psychē. But when we learn that emotions are assigned in the Bible to various bodily organs as their centers, the heart, liver, intestines, for example, we are astonished at the Hebrew's grasp of the fundamental basis of psychosomatic medicine. Neither wholly bodily nor wholly "spiritual," the emotions are the product of the whole person.

Apart from the texts we have studied and referred to, the psalter, the prayerbook of the Bible, gives convincing evidence that biblical man uses his emotions. We can't say that he lives by his emotions, or is emotional, for these expressions mean that he lets his emotions dominate him. But he is emotional in the good sense of making use of them. Because he sees himself as a whole he wouldn't know any other way. Suppressing, and not showing, all emotions is inconceivable to him, and if you tell him that certain cultures inculcate these procedures, he would certainly doubt that these people were sarx and psychē. Biblical man would be a very bad poker player.

I think that some people's way of "talking with their hands" is illustrative here: these people talk with as much of the whole man as possible, and the reason is that the emotions get involved in what they're expressing. Expressing is the word, not talking, for the whole man is communicating, and is, therefore, expressive. This is far more effective and human than the limited way of talking only with the mouth.

A healthy emotional life makes for a healthy spiritual life. This should be quite obvious by now. But let me present a practical example in proof of this, or at least as an illustration. What is called spiritual dryness can result from God's will, God's action purifying our intention, making us seek him for himself alone. It can also result from sin, as well as lukewarmness, from the neglect of God, the dimming of faith, and the lack of supernatural outlook and motivation. But, and this is often not realized, dryness can result from trying to make religion a matter of the soul alone — all intellect and will. When we do this, dryness almost always follows. We are not meant to live in and by intellect and will alone — chiefly, yes, but not as disembodied souls, and when we do, nature kicks back. It is the nature of man to seek and love God as a whole man, and this certainly includes the emotions. We must become emotionally involved with God. I know that "emotionally involved" has another connotation, but I use it deliberately here in order to put over the point. Without the presence of emotions, faith and love run dry, and as a result lukewarmness and the decline of the supernatural set in. We not only have to "stir up the faith" that is in us, but also stir up the emotions, which are very certainly in us. How can we be expected to love God, whom we cannot see without the cooperation of emotions, first and above all others, persons and things, which we do indeed love with the emotions? The emotions are a necessary human aid to love — which, I grant, is essentially an act of the will — and anyone who would counsel otherwise I would suspect of getting letters from Screwtape.

Let me make a suggestion to those who say the divine

office: occasionally give attention to the emotions of the psalms. We have been so formed that attentiveness to the office is to one thing only, the meaning — literal, mystical, or personal — but, nevertheless, to something that is usually intellectual. The praying of the psalms as an intellectual exercise can be a very dessicating experience. From time to time, feel the psalms, really get in there as biblical man and fear, love, shout for joy, and all the rest, without, however, exciting comment. When we pray matins in this way we should come out from it wrung dry emotionally, much as we would after a good melodrama. Not to be recommended every day, but it would make for some pretty memorable matins!

The reason we do not act emotionally in our spiritual life is that we view the emotions with suspicion. One of my senior pupils once asked me if the emotions were good. Even when we realize that they are good we are fearful lest our religion become emotional, which means we fear that it might become all emotion with little thought content. There is more real danger in the opposite happening. What we must avoid is living by the emotions — being directed by them rather than by the intellect and will — and depending on them. Emotions, being psychophysical, come and go, often when we don't want them to. Much depends on the condition of the body, and other circumstances that affect it. We must, in the last analysis, hang on to God by intellect and will, but it needn't be by these two faculties alone. We should summon the help of the emotions, stir up those that are needed. When these fail us, then and then only do we resort to pure intellect and will. God has made us whole, and we must live wholly.

Thus we have an obligation to use our senses. One author refers to them as "our friends." The senses are more than that — our senses are us, for they, too, are sarx and psyche, not just appliances. My eye in the act of seeing is also my psyche seeing, therefore me seeing. As I have said earlier, the eyes, far from being the windows of the soul, are actually the soul made visible. To suppress the life of the senses is to suppress the life of me. The result could be the life of pure intellect and will, which is fine for an angel imprisoned in a human body, but very bad for a human being. I am heartily in favor of custody and mortification of the senses, but not of their death. The method is a matter of penetration, rather than of surface perception. Biblical man always sees through to God.

LIVING SUPERNATURALLY

The problem is not so much living wholly as it is living supernaturally. We have been made aware, by a return to biblical spirituality as well as by the findings of medicine and psychology, of the unity of man. We are less aware than ever of the supernatural direction of man. Now, as never before, must the nature of biblical man be stressed. Expressions such as "secularization" and "involvement in the world" carry dangerous overtones, at the least. Our era may be the "hangover" of the Renaissance, but it is one that is not only lasting a long time but also becoming a crippling malaise.

Biblical man is a unity of sarx and psychē, but he is more than that. He is also pneuma, and therein lies the difference between liberated man of today — and of a long while back — and man as God reveals him to be. When the biblical writers described human life, the psychē, as God's breath, they did not, of course, mean this literally, but expressed in this way the relation of man to God. Sarx-psychē describes man as man, but pneuma treats of the ultimate reason for man. Sarx-psychē tells us the what of man, and his immediate goals; it answers the "Why, daddy?" of the small child. But pneuma alone answers the adult. Sartre and others like him do not know of man as pneuma, only of the incomplete and unsatisfying "flesh." Of course, human existence is at best an enigma, when we don't know the truth about it, when we don't know the answer to the ultimate "why." The only answer, because it is that of God's revealed word, is that man exists because of God and for God. "For God" does describe man's ultimate end, but it includes and demands a day-to-day living that is theocentric. The fullness of revelation in the New Testament completes the answer in concrete detail: God destines man for a physical union with the incarnate Son that results in there being only one man — the whole Christ. Through, in, and with Christ, by the unifying action of the Spirit, we are one with the Father. That, whether we like it or not, is the destiny of man, and literature has often consisted of the bellowings and whimperings of those who haven't liked it. We can no more "de-pneumatize" ourselves than we can rid ourselves of our intellect. To live as if the *pneuma* did not exist is acting like an ostrich.

But you may object, "I have a body and it has needs!" True, but the *pneuma* means that your body's needs have a different meaning, that they are "ultimated." However, the first step to living as God intends is to banish forever the idea that we have or are body and soul. We are *sarx* and *psychē*, and these terms include body and soul but express better the human unity and inter-relationships of biblical man. The next step is to view ourselves, not as a juxtaposition of matter and nonmatter — which we aren't — but as one of nature and supernature, that is, of "flesh" and spirit. From now on I shall use either *flesh* or *sarx* to indicate the natural aspect of man, eliminating *psychē*-soul, because the latter is implied in the former. This procedure is biblical, as we realize. When Paul, for example, opposes the flesh to the spirit, he understands living man. So "spirit," too, implies its existence in the living flesh.

If our Western minds must have a division in man, let it be between the flesh and the spirit, but never between body and soul. For the latter, although different substances, are what make man to be man, hence they are natural to him and not irreconcilable opposites. But flesh and spirit are opposites. They are not irreconcilable, thanks to God's love, but they are as opposite as creature to creator, as finite to infinite, as changing to immutable, as contingent to necessary. For flesh is man and spirit is God. After all, body and soul are each man *in potentia*, but never flesh and spirit. However, you might object, existentially flesh and spirit are also man *in potentia*, for man exists by reason of God's breath, his spirit — man's *psychē* is the *pneuma* of God: hence actual man is flesh and spirit, and cannot be anything else. *Sarx* and *psychē* relate to man, at times even to animals, but they never leave the order of the created. *Pneuma*, on the other hand, is properly God's — his dynamic presence in and on behalf of creation. But man *is* spirit — this is the biblical doctrine. This means, then, that God's dynamic presence is in man to create, orient, and destine; and in the New Testament we realize that man as spirit is a radical capacity for the gift of God's life. Spirit is still God's, even when it is only this capacity, for it is that in man which directs him to God, to be fulfilled only by the reception of God's life. This latter is entirely supernatural to man, beyond the nature, needs, and desserts of the flesh. Hence the real opposition in man is that between the two orders, that of man and that of God, or between the flesh and the spirit.

God created man spirit as well as flesh. That is, he destined man for the supernatural. I think a good illustration of this is the duck, an animal which is destined for water. "He takes to water like a duck," we say of someone who seems to have a natural talent for swimming. The baby duck heads for the water as to its native habitat, waddles in and begins to swim at once. It has an innate orientation to life on the water that makes it effortless, natural, and also necessary. Keep a duck away from water — it will still live, but it will be a frustrated duck. Because he is spirit man tends toward God; he has a natural talent for union with him. He takes to God as a duck takes to water. He may not be aware of this, only that he is restless, unsatisfied, yearning for some nameless, unrecognized thing. He may call it truth, or good, or beauty, or all three. If he does, he's getting through to God. He may try to fill his void by an altruistic love of neighbor. If so, he's on the way. These breakthroughs — breaking through the low horizontal ceiling of the flesh — are like small ponds to the duck. It is made for bigger ones, but these at least are water.

It is at this point, by way of a long parenthesis, that I plead with Christian psychiatrists and psychologists to investigate more deeply the relation between the unconscious and the *pneuma*. Work has already been done. I refer the interested reader to the following books: Lindsay Dewar, *The Holy Spirit and Modern Thought* (New York: Harper and Brothers, 1959); Victor White, O.P., *God and the Unconscious* (Cleveland: The World Publishing Company, 1961); and Josef Goldbrunner, *Individuation* (Notre Dame: University of Notre Dame Press, 1964). Since this is an area in which I have no professional competence, I can only point out what seems to be a real relation, and hope that therapists will take the *pneuma* into account. If man is also spirit, then we must postulate this essential orientation to God, this capacity that can only be filled by God, and take into consideration its demand and need. Not to do so is like misunderstanding the fundamental nature of the duck: like making a nice grassy pen for it, when the poor thing is pining for a pond. Then too, the therapist must at least have a clear intellectual "grasp" of God, and give to his patient the God of the Christians, not some anthropomorphic conception, such as God the Father as a benevolent old man. Rather he must give him God as he is, the unknown God who has revealed himself to a certain extent, and as he has revealed himself. The therapist must be a sound spiritual director, that is, a director of the spirit. To conclude this parenthesis: some years back Miss Mary Pickford wrote a book entitled, *Why Not Try God?* In attempting to cure mental illness we have tried everything else. So why not?

What has been happening in our Western civilization, and the Renaissance was the first large impetus, is elimination of the supernatural. First came the hypothetical elimination by the humanists with their "Let's look at man as he is," which meant merely as *sarx*. From identifying the perceptible with the natural, and the unseen, the "spiritual," with the supernatural, we have come to the mentality of our own day which totally rejects the supenatural because it can't be perceived by the senses. Or rather our mentality eliminates the supernatural because this is an area in which science is not competent, in which it is incapable as science of giving the answers.

But even those who grant the supernatural, who agree with everything I have written in this book so far, can tend to divorce the supernatural from the natural in practice. They make the distinction between religion and "life." These can be very religious people, who go to Mass and receive Communion daily, pray frequently during the day, even make a meditation. But their attitude toward the rest of their day and its secular activities is akin to that of the Renaissance: these are on the natural level, where they rightfully belong, necessary and even enjoyable; they have no intrinsic relation to God, but can be elevated somehow by "offering them up," which offering makes them meritorious. This is what I have called elsewhere[1] split-level living. It is an alternation between the levels of the supernatural and the natural, now up, now down, and a very wearing process it is. A good illustration of this is the typical day of the religious who teaches. His day starts with Mass and prayers. Then off to work in the school. Here he may teach a religion class, then go on to three or four other periods of a purely secular subject. His attitude toward the latter is that it is taught in a more Christian way than it would be in a non-Catholic school, because every now and then he can get in a "plug" for Christianity, and on the whole he teaches it in accord with Catholic doctrine, which often means that he doesn't teach anything heretical or dangerous to faith and morals. His day closes with prayers, recreation, and class preparation. This man is living a split-level life. For although he may be an excellent teacher according to North Central (et al.) standards, he treats his subject as being basically natural. History, for example, no matter what else it is, has one basic meaning for biblical man: it is the account of man's acceptance or rejection of Christ. A mere unit or two of Church history is not going to supernaturalize the whole.

---

[1] Cf. *Led by the Spirit* (Milwaukee: The Bruce Publishing Co., 1965).

To recognize that man is flesh and spirit is not enough. We have to realize the relation of spirit to flesh if we are going to live on the one level, as we should. The spirit of man destines him for God, not his soul only, but his body, too. Since the Bible does not divide man, but regards him whole, spirit is an aspect, a perspective, and, in the last analysis, the *true* aspect of man. This whole, this flesh, is made by God and for God. Therefore a man's most trivial human activities are done for God, because of his very *nature*, not by reason of the "good intention." Because he is a man his life has a religious character — religion is life, rather than opposed to it. This is God's intention in creating man, whether it is *de facto* man's or not. Man is intended to be in all areas of his life a living relation to God. We can say that a person's life is potentially religious, and actually becomes so when he realizes it. Realization results from the knowledge of the true nature of man.

I have taught the biblical doctrine of man to high school boys. Last year one of them painted *pneuma* across the seat of his sweat pants. When I started to object, he defended himself with, "But Father, the whole of me is *pneuma!*" That sentence can save our life, save it from being lived part of the time on the nonexistent natural level. For those of us who are baptized, who are the perfection and completion of biblical man, there is no natural level.

The whole of me is spirit, just as the whole of me is flesh. But the spirit orients, directs the flesh, and in the baptized is joined by the Spirit to Christ. Thus the whole person is truly supernaturalized. The one level that the Christian lives on we can call the supernaturalized natural. He lives a human life, one that is no less in the flesh than that of his good pagan neighbor, but it really belongs to a different order, that of the supernatural. Again we arrive at the unity of biblical man: he is not a dichotomy of body and soul, but a unity of *sarx-psychē*, whereby he can live wholly; he is not an irreconcilable opposition of flesh and spirit, but a unity in which spirit leads. Spirit to spirit enables him to live supernaturally.

CHAPTER 10

Conclusions:
Biblical Man in Incarnopolis

For biblical man there is no secular city. Its existence is no more real than that of Wonderland, Oz, or the Never-never land. He need not retreat to the desert, or to some unspoiled small town. Biblical man can live well-adjusted in the depths, or heights, of the city, immersed in its activity, zooming along its superhighways, enjoying it, but for him it is always, despite its legal name, Incarnopolis — the city of the Logos-become-matter.

Life in Incarnopolis is by no means easy; the incarnational viewpoint has its opponents. Yet biblical man perceives God even in the skyscraper and the most convoluted cloverleaf. He is able to live on the one level of the supernaturalized natural, no matter how many other levels there are in his life, because he lives by faith. But not by faith alone. There is a certainty that the spirit gives which comes from the Holy Spirit: "The Spirit himself gives testimony to our spirit that we are children of God" (Rm 8:16). This certainty is a kind of knowledge — "Now I know in part . . ." (1 Co 13:12) — and when we live by the spirit we know God in his creation. The trick is living by the spirit.

THE SARKICAL CITY

We are surrounded by those who have no sense of the supernatural. The very word, if it belongs to their vocabulary at all, refers only to the occult, to magic, to the unseen preternatural. They take a matter-of-fact attitude toward themselves and their milieu, and look for direction and solace to the science of nature, that is, the natural sciences. They stop at phenomena, accepting these as the total of reality. There is no reality that is not material.

This contemporary attitude can be traced back to that which removed the supernatural from the natural, which admitted that there could be and was, for Christians, a real division between the two. Once this happened, the supernatural was relegated to the realm of the imperceptible, the nonmaterial, and the business of "life" was conducted with the material. Even ideas have finally been assigned to the brain. Religion, then, has become something other than life, over and beyond it, not something deep within and motivating the whole of it. Or if it is an immanent thing, it has ceased to be religion and has ended up as the cult of man. For the Christian, religion is both transcendent and immanent; better, it is transcendence in immanence. The supernatural is radically nonmaterial, true, but — and we must shout this from the house-tops — it permeates matter. This union of the supernatural with matter is like the hypostatic union, and is possible because the Word became matter.

The absence of the sense of the supernatural is really what is called secularization. Harvey Cox has recently described its processes: "The forces of secularization have no serious interest in persecuting religion. Secularization simply bypasses and undercuts religion and goes on to other things. It has relativized religious world-views and thus rendered them innocuous. Religion has been privatized. It has been accepted as the peculiar prerogative and point of view of a particular person or group. . . . The gods of traditional religions live on as private fetishes or the patrons of congenial groups, but they play no role whatever in the public life of the secular metropolis."[1]

This is a sad situation, but it is one which biblical man of today must face, because secularization is his milieu. He must also face the fact that atheism is rampant about him,

---

[1] Harvey Cox, *The Secular City* (New York: The Macmillan Company, 1965), p. 2.

either the professed kind or the implied. This atheism is the most maddening in history because it is based on no logical premises. It seems to take as an *a priori* presumption the fact that God does not exist, and to proceed from there. However, it has one premise, illogical, but convincing enough for contemporary atheists: the self-sufficiency of man. Man can create for himself. He has science, therefore he has no need for God. Therefore God does not exist. Illogical, but the conclusion is with us, at least temporarily.[2]

Secular man today has come to depend on science because his world has been de-supernaturalized. And thus he acquires a certain scientific temper that accepts only the material. He is natural, his world is natural. He is living in the "sarkical" city. This person — and he is all around us — is a failure as a person, because he is more than *sarx* and *psychē*, and his city contains mysteries which are beyond the knowledge and competence of science. The *pneuma* would open up these mysteries. But he is like a little child looking at shelves full of books, which he thinks are only colorful covers that serve as a sort of wall decoration. Someday the child will learn what a book is and how to read it. We must, far from sharing his ignorance or refusing to read, show him what is really *in* a book.

Secularized man, however, need not and often does not live simply a humanized animal life. He can and does pursue truth, good and beauty. His theater, opera, symphony orchestras, libraries, testify to such pursuit. His universities can be most earnest in their seeking truth, and, with their by-product, adult education, witness that he is getting beyond the binding and into the book. But contrasted with the ultimate truth within, such seeking and finding is no better than the reading grasp of the child who is just learning to read. There is so much more to be understood. Life in the *sarx* and the city of the *sarx* is like driving with one foot on the gas and

---

[2] Cf. J. Martin Posadas, S.J., "The Church and Contemporary Atheism: A Historico-Theological Reflection," in *Speaking of God*, ed. by Dennis Derscherl, S.J. (Milwaukee: The Bruce Publishing Co., 1967).

the other on the brake. The car moves, but, as the youngsters say, what a "drag"!

THE WORD BECAME SARX

"The Word became flesh" (Jn 1:14). In English this means that God the Son became a man. But in "Biblical English" the flesh that translates *sarx* here means that the Son became not only a man, but also a relation to the whole of creation. The *sarx* of the incarnate Son fixed him in time and place, made him "locatable," perceptible, with kinship ties, all the things that *sarx* means.

But first let us review our knowledge of the union of the Son with a human nature. We have to keep uppermost John's emphasis that the *Word* took to himself a human nature. The Word is God's creative power, his personified Wisdom, his revelation. This Word is God. He is life and source of life, light and source of light. When he becomes man, he does not cease to be God, for we behold in his humanity the glory of the divinity which he had with the Father before the creation of the world (Jn 1:14; 17:5). His divine Person is also the person of his human nature. The Person of the Word, John tells us, became flesh. From the first instant of the incarnation this Person is the agent of action of his human nature. It is the Word who acts through his human soul and body. Thus the latter belong totally to the Word in a dependence that is vital to their existence and functioning. And thus they are indeed supernaturalized because they are not only endowed and permeated by God, but belong to him to such an extent that they are God. Here, then, we have the greatest and most perfect example of the supernatural as material, as perceptible.

But the body and soul of Jesus are not, for that fact, less real. The evangelists make that clear. Jesus is a genuine human being. And we must realize the fact of his being *sarx*, with all that that means. Jesus has a family, that of David, and humanly speaking is related directly and collaterally to others of that family. He is a Jew, not metaphorically, but truly, with Jewish blood, features, personal traits. He is related to an ethnic group. Sarx makes him one with the whole human race; he belongs to mankind. Every man can call Jesus brother. But sarx does even more than all this: it makes him kin to the whole of material creation.

A man is a microcosm, a union of the elements of the world: he is animal, vegetable, and mineral. And so also is Jesus. He, too, is in some way one with the mountains, plants, and animals. Jesus did more than consecrate the world by his incarnation: he united it to himself, and in himself to his Person of Son. Thus the divine adoption has been extended to all creation. There is a filial character to the world.

The purpose of the incarnation is man's redemption, which means in effect that the Father adopts us as his children through and in Christ. The Spirit unites us to Jesus at the instant of our baptism, puts us into him, and we become one with him. Thus we are by adoption what he is by nature, sons in the Son. We have a share in the divine life which, after death, will develop into the beatific vision. But the point to be emphasized here is our real, physical union with Jesus so that we make up with him, as it were, one Person, the whole Christ. This union is not only with Jesus but also with all those who form his body, so that we, too, are one. Further, our relation to Jesus is similar to the relation of his human nature to his Person of Son — as the Son is the agent of action for his human nature, so Jesus becomes the agent of action for the baptized, because we belong vitally to him, as a knuckle belongs to the person and is under its direction and acts by its will.

The Church, then, is really one Person, and one man, the whole Christ. This is God's intention for man, this is his vision of man. Adam is not the ideal man, but Christ, and Paul simply calls Adam " . . . a figure of him who was to come" (Rm 5:14). To quote again Karl Barth's bold comment on this passage: "Man's essential and original nature is to be found, therefore, not in Adam but in Christ. In Adam we can only find it prefigured. Adam can therefore be interpreted only in the light of Christ and not the other way round."[3] In other words, when the Word became sarx, sarx became the Word, as far as this is possible to creatures. This is the biblical view of man and his fulfilled nature, and we may not take seriously those who in practice divorce man from Christ thus understood.

But the whole Christ is even larger than humanity. He embraces the whole universe. I present here Paul's vision of Christ: "He is the image of the invisible God, the firstborn of every creature. For in him were created all things in the heavens and on the earth, things visible and things invisible, whether Thrones, or Dominations, or Principalities, or Powers. All things have been created through and unto him, and he is before all creatures, and in him all things hold together. Again, he is the head of his body, the Church; he, who is the beginning, the firstborn from the dead, that in all things he may have the first place. For it has pleased God the Father that in him all his fullness should dwell, and that through him he should reconcile to himself all things, whether on the earth or in the heavens, making peace through the blood of his cross" (Col 1:15–20; Kleist-Lilly tr.).

In the eternal knowledge of God all creation was intended for Christ, to be taken into the whole Christ. The mystery of the Father's will " . . . he decreed to put into effect in Christ when the designated period of time had elapsed, namely to gather all creation both in heaven and on earth under one head, Christ" (Eph 1:9–10; Kleist-Lilly tr.). The Greek here is literally translated "to head all things in Christ," which means that by his death, resurrection, and ascension, the effects of the redemption have come down and gone out to all creatures, to gather them up into his Person. This will be fully accomplished at Christ's second coming: "For I reckon that the sufferings of the present time are not worthy to be compared with the glory to come that will be revealed in us. For the eager longing of creation awaits the

---

[3] Karl Barth, *Christ and Adam* (New York: Collier Books, 1962), pp. 39–40.

revelation of the sons of God. For creation was made subject to vanity — not by its own will but by reason of him who made it subject — in hope, because creation itself also will be delivered from its slavery to corruption into the freedom of the glory of the sons of God. For we know that all creation groans and travails in pain until now. And not only it, but we ourselves also who have the first-fruits of the Spirit — we ourselves groan within ourselves, waiting for the adoption as sons, the redemption of our body" (Rm 8:18–23; Kleist-Lilly tr.). Paul's cosmic vision is of the whole of creation, human and nonhuman, forming the body of Christ; this is Teilhard's unity from multiplicity, akin to Plato's one from the many.

The vision is eschatalogical, but the kingdom of heaven has already begun. The beatific vision is already present in sanctifying grace; adoption began at baptism. Hence, creation is daily being taken into the whole Christ. How? By the touch of Christ upon it. The Christian is the touch of Christ on creation, he is the hand which the head uses, to reach, to take up, to fashion and make. The Christian's use of creation, *acting as Christ*, takes it into the whole Christ. He is creation's contact with Christ, similar to the hem of his garment through which power flows.

This means that the Christian's view of creation is that of Christ. Christ's view is based on the cosmic fact that all creation belongs to him. This is easier to grasp when we think of creation as nature in the natural state. The Christian beholding the mountains, great forests, canyons, has little difficulty realizing that all of these were created by and for the Word. But the skyscrapers, the supermarkets, space capsules, and television, belong to Christ as well. They were ultimately created by and for him. When the Christian looks at the city, he must exclaim, "All this is Christ's." And more, he must daily realize that all this must be taken into the body, the *sarx*, of Christ. The *sarx* that the Son became, forever, henceforth, belongs to him, and must be united to him, not simply the *sarx* of his own human nature, but the whole kinship of *sarx* — the whole of mankind, with the settings in which men live out their humanity, and the things that they need to be human. So the Christian beholding the city sees it not only as Christ's, but as an extension of Christ.

So nature is not meant to be pure nature, but supernature, as man is meant to be Christ. Therefore, matter is destined for the supernatural: part of the realm of the *sarx*, it is meant to be joined to the *sarx* of the Son. The supernatural is supposed to permeate matter, to elevate and use it. And when matter is so elevated and used the supernatural becomes visible, perceptible. Just as the things belonging to someone we love make him present, and we are able to say that he is there by means of his pipe, his chair, his books, so every object that Christ uses through our use makes him present through the object.

So the city is Incarnopolis to the Christian, and, sad to say, merely Technopolis to secularized man. Both live there, in the same apartment building, both shop in the same huge stores, drive similar cars, watch the same television programs; but one sees the surfaces, contacts the immediate, or mediate; the other sees and contacts Christ.

Living by the Spirit

The spirit of man orients him to union with God, makes him a capacity for God. The New Testament teaching regarding man makes the role of the spirit and the nature of this union more specific, as well as quite definite: the spirit is a man's point of contact with the Trinity's "point" of contact, the Holy Spirit, who unites him to the body of Christ. Hence, because of his spirit, a man is an orientation to this physical union with Christ, which is achieved by the Spirit. Every man is meant to be in Christ, and, therefore, as far as this is possible to a creature, to be Christ. His spirit drives him to this completion of his humanity, to the fulfillment of his person by the Person of the Son. Because he is spirit, he is restless and frustrated until he becomes Christ.

To live by the spirit — what is called the spiritual life — is to live as Christ. It is not "the life of the soul," but a life that is supernatural. And since the spirit is a necessary aspect of man as man, it is proof that he is destined for the supernatural.

Living by the spirit is letting Christ live in his creation, in his world, whether this is in the city, suburb, or country. Christ relives and continues his own life in the world before his ascension through each part of his body, each Christian, no matter how recently grafted into him it is — he works, preaches, suffers — giving the Father the glory of his love.

When the Christian lives by his spirit, he goes out of himself, out of his selfish and horizontal interests, desires, and fears, to Christ. He ceases to live as sarx, as just a human being. He seeks and finds Christ, constantly. Thus he is prevented from being self-absorbed, a person in-drawn, wrapped up in himself, conquered by his fears. He gives himself rather to the interests of Christ — to what Christ wants to do with him, and his time. If only a man will let his own spirit direct his life, or, rather, the Spirit acting on his spirit!

He would go out to Christ in "the other," his neighbor, especially when the other is a Christian, for he would find Christ in him. And when he is not, he would see him as a potential part of the body of Christ, and anticipate the event by his attitude and efforts. The spirit of man impels him to love. Love is the basic human emotion, another proof of the existence of the spirit of man. The sarx is self-centered, and when it loves it does so with the imperfect, immature love of the child, the love that desires not to give but to get. Hence the sarx is not the complete man. The spirit loves with the love of benevolence, and the Spirit directs it to Christ in the other. Thus the Christian's life is centered, not so much on others, but on the Other, and the second great commandment becomes, in effect, the same as the first.

The Son became sarx, and thus incarnated himself in all those human beings who receive him. He is extended throughout the extent of the world, including all those whose head he is. Each Christian is a new flesh for the Son. The sarx implies a human, not an angelic, way of life, which means life in the world, and this life, too, as we have seen, must be taken into Christ. But what about the world? Isn't it an evil thing from which Christ wished to be disassociated? "I am praying for them; I am not praying for the world but for those whom thou hast given me, for they are thine. . . . I have given them thy word; and the world has hated them because they are not of the world, even as I am not of the world" (Jn 17:9, 14), he said to the Father.

The "world" does not mean God's creation, but the secular city, creation considered apart from God, creation divorced from God, either explicitly or in practice. A "worldly" person is not one who enjoys life in the world, but one who does so with no reference to God. When we regard creation as belonging to Christ, and as clamoring to be used as Christ wills to use it, we are a million light-years from those who see it as existing solely for man, no matter how much a sacred trust from God it is seen to be. Great as man is, he is still merely man — flesh, as against God who is spirit — and using creation for mere man belongs to an infinitely lower order than using it for God, or, to be more precise, for God become man and the kin of all creation.

To continue with Christ's prayer: "And now I am no more in the world, but they are in the world, and I am coming to thee. Holy Father, keep them in thy name, which thou hast given me, that they may be one, even as we are one. . . . I do not pray that thou shouldst take them out of the world, but that thou shouldst keep them from the evil one. They are not of the world, even as I am not of the world. . . . As thou didst send me into the world, so I have sent them into the world" (Jn 17:11, 15-16, 18).

The apostles, and after them all Christians, are to be the continuation of the incarnation in the world — the presence and activity of Christ. Their way of life is that of the Trinity, one in the Son, and in him, one with the Father, and all this the work of the Spirit. They are not "of the world," that is, purely natural, living in the flesh, no more than was

Christ, whose humanity was and is totally supernaturalized by its union with the Son. And as extensions of Christ, their place is in the world. May I point out to those who erroneously see "involvement" in the world as rather a complete submersion in it, the terms of Christian involvement? The Christian goes to the world as sent, and, if he is a priest or religious, sent by the interpreter of the Father's will for him, his ecclesiastical superior. Then, he is sent as Christ, not as himself, to give self, the *sarx* with all its demands and hankerings, to Christ to let *him* accomplish the work of *his* mission. Only on these terms can the priest and religious become involved in the world.

There is a term much prized by Secular Institutes, because it expresses their whole purpose and genius, and this is *secularity*. *Secularity* means holiness in the world and *by means of the world*. Members of Secular Institutes profess poverty, chastity, and obedience, the life of perfection; they give themselves completely to Christ with the same dedication and spirit of renunciation as religious do, but all of this is set in the milieu of the world, as against the religious house. The world is to be their means of perfection: they do not enter a monastery or convent in order to keep the vows of poverty, chastity, and obedience; they stay in the world in order to keep these counsels. The papal document *Primo Feliciter* is emphatic on this point: " . . . it must always be borne in mind that the proper and peculiar character of such Institutes, namely that they are *secular* — and in this lies the whole reason for the existence of such Institutes — must stand out clearly in everything. Nothing of the full profession of Christian perfection, solidly based on the evangelical counsels and truly religious as to its substance, will be withdrawn, but this perfection is to be exercised and professed *in the world*; and consequently, it must be adapted to secular life in all such things as are lawful and not opposed to its duties and exercise. . . . This Apostolate of the Secular Institutes is to be faithfully exercised not only *in the world* but as originating *from the world* and, consequently, through those professions, occupations, jobs and in places and circumstances corresponding to this secular condition."[4]

Secular Institutes lead the way for the layman, just as they give the lie to the erroneous belief that those who are a part of life in the world and enjoy the experience are worldly. Secularity is necessary for biblical man who, though not consecrated to God by the profession of the evangelical counsels, is indeed radically consecrated by his baptism and confirmation, and is thereby bound to profess the full life of Christ in Christ's world. The decree on the lay apostolate of the Second Vatican Council has this injunction: "In regard to the Christian renewal of the temporal order, the laity should be instructed in the true meaning and value of temporal things, both in themselves and in relation to all the aims of the human person. They should be trained in the right use of things and the organization of institutions. . . ."[5] Biblical man, by means of secularity, uses the world as much as or even more than does secularized man, and with what a difference in depth and fulfillment!

Secularized man lives only in the flesh (or *sarx-psychē*), biblical man, in the spirit, which includes, of course, the flesh. It is true that urban living hides ultimate causality, and, at times, makes it implausible. The atmosphere, let's face it, is the natural, and even the unnatural. Secularized man sees only the natural: this is the city of man, created by and for man. But the spirit of man "ultimates" him, gives him perception, the vision of the ultimate creator. When we see a building designed by a famous architect, we say, for example, "That building is by Frank Lloyd Wright." We know very well that Wright didn't *build* the structure, but conceived it mentally and put his ideas and mental picture down on his drawing board. Mediate causes then put the result into concrete execution. So biblical man looks at the city and by means of his spirit sees the causality of God, and only

---

[4] Salvador Canals, *Secular Institutes and the State of Perfection* (Dublin: Scepter Ltd., 1959), pp. 158–159.
[5] *Decree on the Lay Apostolate*, no. 31.

then the causality of man. Biblical man looks for, and is able to perceive God, by reason of his spirit. It is the way of the incarnation: he doesn't stop at the human nature of Jesus Christ, but goes beyond to the person of the Son; so he doesn't stop at the world of the flesh, but gets within to the Word who assumed it. The great secret of living by the spirit is not to stop at the flesh, but to penetrate to Christ.

Living by the spirit is in reality living by the Holy Spirit, or, what we might call living by his seven gifts. The doctrine of the gifts depends on this text of Isaiah: "The Spirit of the Lord shall rest upon him, the spirit of wisdom and understanding, the spirit of counsel and might, the spirit of knowledge and the fear of the Lord, and his delight shall be in the fear of the Lord" (Is 11:2). The Septuagint has *eusebeia*, piety, instead of the first fear of the Lord. Isaiah is referring here to the Messiah; hence, the Church concludes that the Spirit gives the same gifts to the Christian, who is physically united to him.

To understand the gifts and living by them we must recall the relation of the *ruach* to the prophet. The latter is a man of the spirit of the Lord, because by means of the spirit he is enabled to receive God's word. The spirit puts him into an ecstasy, and in this ecstasy he receives the word. Without the spirit of the Lord he is not a prophet. We must keep this well in mind.

Jesus, the evangelists insist, is a prophet. He is the man of the Spirit, who invests him with his messianic mission, leads and impels him throughout his public life. His religion is to be charismatic, one of personal dependence on the Spirit, for he baptizes with the Spirit, and thus gives him to his followers. We know from several New Testament texts that it was the Holy Spirit who was the prophet's *ruach* of the Lord.

Thus, filled with the Spirit, the Christian, too, is a prophet. The Church can only begin to exist when the Spirit comes upon the apostles at Pentecost, and upon the newly baptized, in turn, for the Christian is a man of the Spirit. This phenomenon results from his union with Christ, but it is not a mere by-product. If a person is to be a Christian, it is absolutely necessary that he be charismatic — that the Spirit lead and impel him, as he did the prophets, and, later, Christ. The prophetic character of the Christian is not the viewpoint of a school of spirituality; it is an unassailable fact.

Because the Christian abides in Christ, in his body, the Spirit abides in him. The Spirit's visitations are not fitful, or rare, as was sometimes the case in the Old Testament. Therefore the Spirit is present for action, daily and even hourly action, and the Christian must see his life as not so much personal effort as cooperation. The gifts are so many powers enabling the person to receive the action of the Spirit. Or, more precisely, the gifts are the Spirit, disposing the person to receive seven different kinds of prophetic "words." They are not the words themselves, but are akin to the ecstasy which the Spirit induced in the prophet. When the Christian is thus disposed, then the Spirit gives the word. We have to remember the way in which the prophet received the word of God, and the nature of that word — not the prophet's, but God's, given to him by the Spirit. The Spirit by means of the gifts works precisely the same way. The person does nothing but be receptive. The Spirit gives the word. Only then does the person act — he recognizes the action of the Spirit, realizes his obligation, and follows through, by the aid of actual grace. That is why I call the Christian life a cooperation.[6]

If this all seems too supernatural, may I point out that Christianity is a supernatural religion, and it takes a doctrine such as that of the gifts to bring out the fact. I think that the reason Christianity has failed to permeate the lives of great masses of Christians, to influence their attitudes, is that the supernatural has either not been stressed, or else not been rightly taught. The fact of the one level of living,

[6] For a detailed treatment of the gifts, see my A Synthesis of the Spiritual Life (Milwaukee: The Bruce Publishing Company, 1962), pp. 215-274.

the supernaturalized natural, the fact of biblical man — are these taught, and, if they are, are they understood? Do they get through to Christians?

To return to the gifts: how much simpler and easier, and more in accordance with man's true nature, life would be if it were lived as a daily cooperation with the Spirit. To believe that the effort has to be ours, with the help of grace, is not a Christian attitude. It is one step above good Stoic living, rather like Seneca with Christian footnotes. The phrases "acquisition of virtue," and "striving for perfection" are good, as far as they go, but of themselves they lead to an enervating dryness, discouragement, and giving up, except for certain choleric natures. The seven "virtues" are *infused*, and while we must take the power that they give and perform acts of the virtues, we must remember that the power is *given* to us. Even though this power is supernatural, the life of the virtues is difficult. It is only when the Spirit acts by means of the gifts that we can ease up on the oars, to use John of St. Thomas' example, and let the Spirit — the Pentecostal wind — in the sails power our boat.

The Spirit acts upon our spirit daily, and frequently in the day. In fact, our spirit is attuned to him, to his voice. When we hear his words, and act on them, accept his leading, see creation in his vision, when every moment becomes a Spirit-to-spirit cooperation, we reach that peace which not only exceeds understanding, but is not its product, because it is only given by the Spirit as the condition and reward for living as God intends man to live.

Subject Index

and love, 117, 119 f; love aspect of man, 142; of man and supernatural, 53; in New Testament, 87 ff; and *nous*, 109 f; in Old Testament, 71 ff; orients to God, 65, 79 ff, 98, 102, 106 ff, 120, 137 f, 139, 150 ff; and person, 145; power from God, 76 ff; prophetic in layman, 81 f; and prophets, 111 ff; and psychology, 140; in reality God's, 76 ff; relation to God, 104 ff; and sanctifying grace, 122; and *scintilla animae*, 108 f; similarity with soul, 75; and soul, 82 ff, 85, 100 f; 131 f; and spirit of God, 82; summary of biblical doctrine, 129 f; and supernatural, 29 f; supernatural faculty, 104, 105 ff; supernatural power, 78 f; supernatural principle, 98; and truth, 121; and unconscious, 140; and understanding, 80 f; and union with God, 108 f; and vitality, 72; whole man, 142; whole person, 131

Spirit of God, as abiding, 66 ff; as creative, 62 ff; and God's presence, 54; and God's word, 64; and grace of state, 76; and Holy Spirit, 92; and judges, 55 f; and kings, 56; and Messiah, 69 f; and mind, 54 f; in Old Testament, 53 ff; as power, 54 ff; and his presence, 68 f; and prophets, 56 ff, 67 f, 155; and re-creation, 63 f, 88, 118 f

Spiritual life, 126 ff, 150 ff

Supernatural, and natural, 131, 141 f, 143 ff; and spirit, 29 f; and spirit of man, 53

Supernatural living, 137 ff

Torah, and Holy Spirit, 95

Truth, and spirit, 121

Unconscious, and spirit, 140

Union with God, and spirit, 108 f

World, 152 ff

Biblical Index

163